DINOSAUR
A - Z

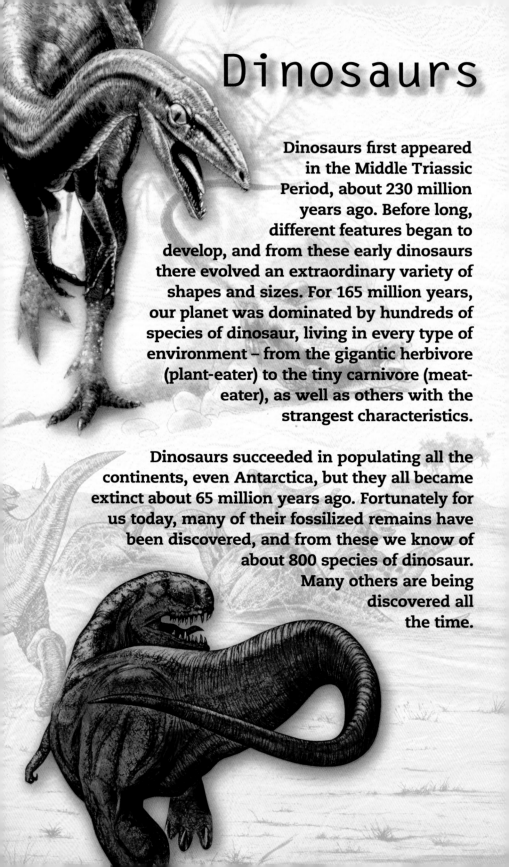

Dinosaurs

Dinosaurs first appeared in the Middle Triassic Period, about 230 million years ago. Before long, different features began to develop, and from these early dinosaurs there evolved an extraordinary variety of shapes and sizes. For 165 million years, our planet was dominated by hundreds of species of dinosaur, living in every type of environment – from the gigantic herbivore (plant-eater) to the tiny carnivore (meat-eater), as well as others with the strangest characteristics.

Dinosaurs succeeded in populating all the continents, even Antarctica, but they all became extinct about 65 million years ago. Fortunately for us today, many of their fossilized remains have been discovered, and from these we know of about 800 species of dinosaur. Many others are being discovered all the time.

Editorial Co-ordination: Stefano Sibella
Graphics, pagination and cover: Viviana Cerrato
Picture research: Paola D'Agostino, Viviana Cerrato
Technical Manager: Gianluigi Ronchetti

Photographs and drawings: DeA Picture Library; Davide Bonadonna –
cover and pages 40–41, 54–55, 61, 68, 70–71, 73, 77, 81 (top), 88–89,
107 (Dino Quiz), 109 (top), 115, 119 (Dino Quiz), 122–123, 124–125, 127
(top), 131 (top), 137, 143 (Dino Quiz), 150, 174–175, 185 (Dino Quiz),
188–189, 210, 212–213, 214–215, 218–219, 220–221, 228, 228–229,
242–243, 251 (bottom)

Special thanks to:
Nando Musmarra and Diana Fattori for the photographs on pages 21,
22 and 41 (centre); the pictures on page 72 and on pages 90–91 are by
Serguio Pezzoli (EVOLUTION).

English edition translated from the Italian by Maureen Spurgeon
and Rosetta Translations
Edited by Gill Davies

ISBN: 978-0-7097-1828-4

Dinosauri dalla A alla Z
© 2007 Istituto Geografico De Agostini S.p.A., Novara
© 2008 Brown Watson, English edition

Contents

Fossils and Fossilization

A fossil is the remains of any living thing which existed on Earth in ancient times. The word 'fossil' comes from the Latin verb *födere*, which means 'to dig'. Each fossil is evidence of a world which has now disappeared – all that remains of a plant or an animal which became extinct long, long ago. Some fossils may be quite complete, such as the scales of a reptile, or the fronds of a fern. Other fossils may comprise just skeletons and bones, or footprints, nests, eggs … in fact, anything which a creature or plant has left behind as evidence of its time on Earth.

The process of fossilization

Fossilization is a rare but, natural process – most dead organisms from ancient times were not preserved. It is the result of a complex series of chemical and physical processes. The ideal conditions for fossilization occur when the remains of an organism are buried quickly under a thick layer of mud, sand or other sediment. When a fossil is unearthed, its location helps us to establish where the organism lived, often in prehistoric lakes, seas, swamps and the larger rivers. A quick burial helps to preserve the whole organism – because, the more its remains come into contact with the air, the quicker these will disintegrate. Also, once the remains of the dead organism are under the sediments, they cannot be attacked by predators or swept away by currents of water. Over millions of years, the layers of sediment become rocks which build up one on top of another, creating the thick covering which encloses the 'future fossils'. This is the reason why fossils are so big and heavy when they are chipped out of their rocky hiding places.

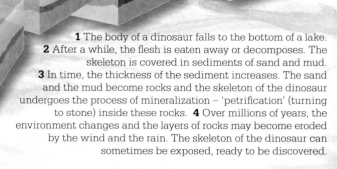

1 The body of a dinosaur falls to the bottom of a lake. **2** After a while, the flesh is eaten away or decomposes. The skeleton is covered in sediments of sand and mud. **3** In time, the thickness of the sediment increases. The sand and the mud become rocks and the skeleton of the dinosaur undergoes the process of mineralization – 'petrification' (turning to stone) inside these rocks. **4** Over millions of years, the environment changes and the layers of rocks may become eroded by the wind and the rain. The skeleton of the dinosaur can sometimes be exposed, ready to be discovered.

8

At the same time, water has been filtering in through the rocks, seeping into the remains of the organism and leaving behind deposits of mineral salts. These mineral salts also help to preserve the cells of the organism, so that it keeps its original appearance – its shape and structure. This process is called 'mineralization'. It takes millions of years until the remains become fossilized in this way.

After that, erosion by wind and rain gradually wears away the layers of rock, bringing the fossilized organism to light.

The work of palaeontology

Palaeontology is the study of fossils – and because fossils have been enclosed in rock for millions and millions of years, excavating them is very hard work for the palaeontologists. As well as the size of a fossil, which may be quite considerable, palaeontologists often have to stay in remote locations away from airports and railways, in places which are difficult to reach. Almost immediately a fossil is brought to light, the palaeontologist must try to determine what bone it is and whether there may be other parts of the limb or the skeleton nearby. At this point, the newly-found fossil must be delicately and carefully removed from the rocks which surround it. Depending on the type of material, different instruments are used; hammers and chisels for hard rocks, brushes for softer and looser sediment. The next step is to prepare each fossil so that it is protected during its journey to the museum. Usually, it is wrapped in damp paper and then covered by bandages, strips of paper or pieces of material soaked in plaster. This plaster, once it is dry, forms a rigid case around the remains which palaeontologists call a 'jacket'. The fossil, in its jacket, is then taken to the museum for further preparation. This includes cleaning it thoroughly and freeing it from the rock. Various instruments are used to do this – drills, steel points, scalpels, very fine needles and jets of air and sand for more delicate removal. Sometimes acid has to be used to dissolve the rocks around the fossil. Then, once the various parts are freed from the rock, they have to be put together, rather like a jigsaw puzzle. Missing pieces are often rebuilt, using plastic resin. Now the fossil is ready to be catalogued, classified and described by palaeontologists in every detail.

Above: a group of palaeontologists searching for fossils among layers of rocks.

Left: fossilized bones of a dinosaur preserved in rock.

First Discoveries and Recent Theories

In the early 1800s, William Buckland, Professor of Geology at Oxford University, came into the possession of a small collection of fossilized bones – a jaw with long, sharp, jagged teeth and the bones of limbs, ribs and vertebrae. Buckland studied these bones and came to the conclusion that they were the remains of an enormous extinct reptile which was later called *Megalosaurus*. Buckland's description of this huge creature was published in 1824. It was the first scientific publication on dinosaurs.

The second dinosaur was discovered by Mary Ann Mantell at Lewes, in Sussex, near the south coast of England. While out walking, she picked up some fossilized teeth which she showed to her husband, Gideon Mantell. He was a doctor as well as a geologist and very interested in fossils. He examined them and decided that the teeth his wife had found were similar to those of the iguana, a lizard from Central America – but much, much bigger. He established that these fossilized remains must have belonged to an extinct reptile similar to a gigantic iguana and which Mantell named *Iguanodon*, meaning 'teeth of an iguana'.

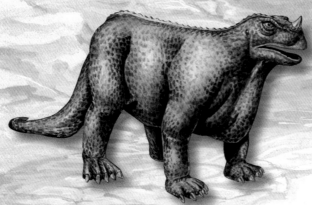

Left: an old reconstruction of an *Iguanodon*.

Opposite page, top: illustration to explain the theory of a single strand of evolution, starting with the thecodont (meaning 'teeth in sockets') reptiles, leading on to dinosaurs and then to birds. **centre:** the American palaeontologist Robert Bakker.

Megalosaurus and *Iguanodon* were dinosaurs – but it was the great palaeontologist Richard Owen who gave them that name. Owen knew they were reptiles but quite different to those now on Earth – enormous and with straight legs underneath the body; an extinct group of reptiles but more developed than any existing reptiles. In 1841, Owen invented a new name for these monsters of the past – *Dinosauria*, which in ancient Greek means 'terrible lizards'.

From clumsy, slow reptiles of the past to modern dinosaurs

In 1969, the American palaeontologist John Ostrom described the remains of the *Deinonychus*, a meat-eating dinosaur similar to the *Velociraptor* but much bigger. In the course of his studies, Ostrom realized that he was examining the remains of a creature which nobody could ever have believed was a reptile. The agile, fast *Deinonychus* did not

have strong jaws and in all probability after catching its prey with its long arms, killed it with its legs and claws. The *Deinonychus* had a deadly weapon – a long claw in the shape of a scythe on the second 'toe' of each foot and which it used both to keep its balance and to catch and cut into its prey. This method of attack was quite different to any of the larger meat-eating dinosaurs but Ostrom's studies signalled the beginning of modern palaeontology and a new vision of dinosaurs. Now, they were no longer seen as clumsy, slow animals but creatures able to run, to balance and to flee at high speed – in fact, a lifestyle not unlike that of birds and animals today. In 1860 the first fossilized remains of an *Archaeopteryx* were discovered – a bird with a tail, teeth and claws similar to a dinosaur's. This discovery led to many debates (which still continue among palaeontologists), as to the relationship between dinosaurs and birds – the similarity in the structure of these animals is so strong. Since then and especially in recent years, there have been many more astounding discoveries, many giving more

evidence to support the theory of a single strand of evolution, starting with the thecodont reptiles, passing on to dinosaurs and then to birds. In 1975, the American palaeontologist Robert Bakker, a disciple of Ostrom, came up with a new theory. He maintained that, whereas other reptiles were cold-blooded (their body temperature depending on their surroundings), dinosaurs were warm-blooded, able to produce heat from within their own body and so maintain a constant body temperature. This was the beginning of a long debate. The question – were dinosaurs cold-blooded or warm-blooded? – is still being argued and so far, no firm agreement has been reached.

CLASSIFICATION OF DINOSAURS

Dinosaurs are classified as vertebrates – because, like all vertebrates, a dinosaur had an internal skeleton supported by a vertebral column (or spine). The class of vertebrates includes fishes, amphibians, reptiles, birds and mammals. Today, dinosaurs are classed as reptiles but there is no doubt that in coming years, as more fossilized remains come to light, this classification will be re-examined. In fact, there are many ways in which dinosaurs differ from reptiles, the most significant difference being with regard to the bones in the feet, legs and hips.

As a reptile moves, it keeps its legs bent and sticking out at either side of its body. As it goes along, its stomach grazes the ground, its spine moving from right to left, left to right and its claws completing the whole, wide semi-circular movement. On the other hand, a dinosaur's legs were straight and underneath its body (like a dog or a cow), so that its stomach and tail did not touch the ground as it ran along. In common with birds, dinosaurs had 'digits' (finger-like claws). A dinosaur did not put its whole foot on the ground, only the claw. The pelvis, which comprised the

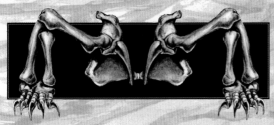

ilium, ischium and pubis, was very strong and fused to the sacral (rear back) vertebrae to give it added strength. This structure of the legs and the pelvis is found in many groups of biped dinosaurs (those moving on their hind legs).

Saurischia and Ornithischia

Dinosaurs can be divided into two main groups, based on the position of the bones in the pelvis – the *Saurischia* or 'lizard-hips' with the pubis facing to the front and the ischium towards the back; and the *Ornithischia* or 'bird-hips', in which both the pubis and the ischium turn inward, towards the back. The sauropods – gigantic herbivore (plant-eating) four-legged dinosaurs and the theropods – biped carnivore (meat-eating) dinosaurs of different sizes – both belonged to the Saurischian group. Among the Ornithischians, we find only herbivore dinosaurs, both biped and four-legged.

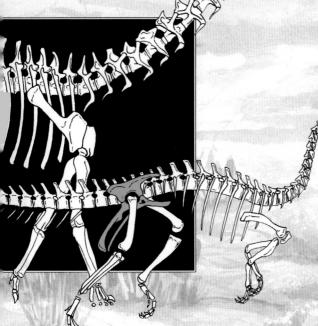

Left: reptiles move with their limbs bent and sticking out from the body.

Above: the legs of reptiles today are bent and positioned at the sides of the body; a dinosaur's legs were straight and positioned directly under the body.

Left: the pelvis of Saurischian dinosaurs, such as the giant *Camarasaurus*, was structured in such a way that the pubis faced forward and the ischium backward. Ornithischian dinosaurs, such as the smallest and most agile *Camptosaurus*, had both pubis and ischium turned inward, facing towards the back.

Eras and Dinosaurs

The study of fossils has given us lots of evidence about the progressive and complex evolution both of our planet and life on Earth. This knowledge has enabled scientists to sub-divide geological times into intervals, based on particular biological or geological events which have affected the development of the Earth – such as the proof of extinction or the appearance of new species. There are four main stages which we call Eras. Each of these Eras is divided into shorter periods of time – we call these Periods.

ERA	PERIOD	MILLLIONS OF YEARS AGO
Cenozoic	Quaternary	2
	Terziary	65
Mesozoic	Cretaceous	146
	Jurassic	208
	Triassic	250
Paleozoic	Permian	290
	Carboniferous	362
	Devonian	408
	Silurian	439
	Ordovician	510
	Cambrian	550
Archeozoic	Proterozoic	1000
	Archaean	4560

The geological Eras are sub-divided into Periods. These sub-divisions should be read from the bottom to the top, because the oldest rocks are beneath those which are younger.

Opposite page, centre: Conifers, (the group to which today's pine and fir trees belong) were among the most common plants in the Mesozoic Era.
Ferns (centre) are considered 'living fossils' because they have hardly changed since the Mesozoic Era.
Cycadaceae (centre right) were also very common. These were similar to palms but with short, thick stems. They are very rare today.
A fossilized conifer (bottom, right).

The Mesozoic Era was the age when the dinosaurs ruled the Earth. It was also the time when the first mammals and birds began to appear. These would be the ancestors of species in each Era that followed.

The Mesozoic Era was dominated by reptiles of various kinds. They fed on anything, from small animals to insects and plants. The most well-established of these reptiles were the Thecodonts, their legs almost completely straight and their strong teeth firmly fixed into their jawbones. Dinosaurs originated from Thecodonts.

14

At the dawn of the Mesozoic or dinosaur Era, in the **Triassic Period**, there was just one huge land mass, called the Pangaea, surrounded by one vast ocean (the Panthalassa). The Pangaea had no high mountain ranges – so there were no land barriers and the first dinosaurs were able to migrate long distances, from one part of the Earth to another, always in a warm climate. Some parts of the Pangaea were dry and covered by enormous deserts; other areas had a tropical climate and were covered by forests of evergreen plants such as conifers, ferns and cycadaceae. The Pangaea began to break up towards the end of the **Jurassic Period**, about 140 million years ago. At first, it became two vast land masses, Laurasia to the north and Gondwana to the south, with the Tethys Sea in between. The climate of the Jurassic Period became less dry. Rainy seasons alternated with drier periods and lush tropical forests covered the Earth, criss-crossed by rivers,

lakes and swamps in which lived species of reptiles that became ever bigger. This lush environment allowed dinosaurs to 'explode' in to thousands of new species.

The Earth's land masses continued to break up during the **Cretaceous Period**. The Atlantic and Indian Oceans began opening up and the continents started to look very much the same shapes as they are today.

The Mesozoic Era ended in a dramatic way. 65 million years ago, some disaster happened which brought about the extinction of many living things on the planet. This meant that the survivors, including mammals and birds, could live and develop on Earth, without any threat from the dinosaurs which had been the ruling class for so long. This was the start of a new chapter in the story of life on Earth.

NON-DINOSAURS

Many other reptiles lived on Earth at the same time as dinosaurs but were less important. Dinosaurs had survived for millions of years, living almost everywhere, from huge swamps to dense forests and in all climates. They were the ruling class. Synapsida, the group of reptiles from which mammals originated, lived alongside dinosaurs on land.

Marine reptiles

The warm ocean waters of the Mesozoic Era were home to some strange creatures with long necks, shells or armour plating and flippers. These were the placodonts, plesiosaurs and ichthyosaurs. None of these have left descendants. Like dinosaurs, these creatures became extinct.

The ichthyosaur was similar to today's dolphin with a hydrodynamic body (shaped to move through water) no neck but a long, thin nose, numerous sharp teeth, fins and a strong tail to propel it along. The largest ichthyosaurs, up to 15 metres long, lived at the end of the Triassic Period. These were the most primitive (least developed) with no dorsal fins but with a long tail; by the Jurassic Period, the ichthyosaur had dorsal fins and a tail in the shape of a crescent moon. It ate fish, molluscs and cephalods (such as ammonites and prehistoric squid), which the ichthyosaur would catch easily as it swam along. An ichthyosaur could also take deep breaths which it could hold for a long time. It had enormous eyes which were so well developed that it could see perfectly, swimming at great depths without losing any vision.

Ichthyosaurs could not leave the sea to lay their eggs; the females kept the eggs in their abdomens until they were ready to be hatched. Then they gave birth directly in the sea. This extraordinary creature became extinct towards the mid-Cretaceous Period.

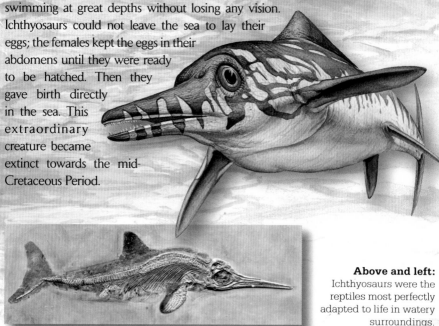

Above and left:
Ichthyosaurs were the reptiles most perfectly adapted to life in watery surroundings.

16

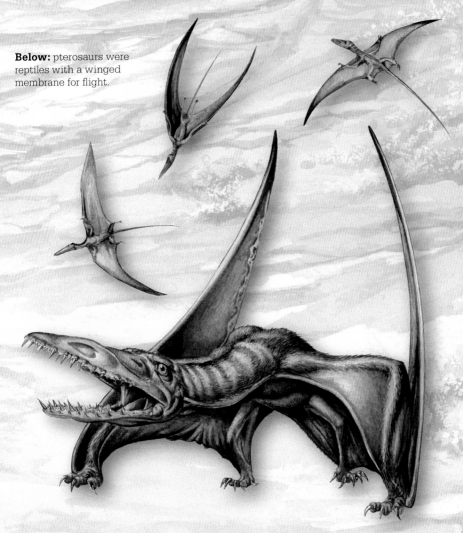

Below: pterosaurs were reptiles with a winged membrane for flight.

Flying reptiles

Pterosaurs were the first vertebrates which could fly. They appeared at the end of the Triassic Period and eventually developed a body structure which was almost perfect for flying. A splendid, aerodynamic (shaped for flight) crest appeared on the skull and an extra tail section acted like a rudder for steering. Hollow bones made its body lighter.

During the Mesozoic Era, many pterosaur species developed – the smallest was the size of a dove, the largest as big as a jet aircraft. But a pterosaur was not a bird. Its wings were membranes of stretchy thin, strong skin, without plumage or feathers, joined to the sides of the body and held up only by an extremely long fourth 'finger'. Its first three 'fingers' were short but with claws spreading out from the inside edge of the wing.

Most flying reptiles lived near lakes, streams, rivers or shallow seas, feeding on fish, molluscs and insects.

17

EXTiNCTiON

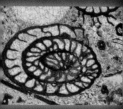

After having dominated the Earth for the whole of an Era, all the dinosaurs disappeared, perhaps in the space of a few thousand years. In the rocks which formed 65 million years ago, after the Cretaceous Period, there are no traces of dinosaurs – not a bone, a tooth, the tiniest fragment of eggshell, or a footprint.

Not only had dinosaurs disappeared by the end of the Cretaceous Period but also many other forms of life – flying reptiles, marine reptiles, many groups of birds and marsupial mammals, some groups of fish and ammonites, as well as microscopic one-celled organisms such as foraminifera and radiolaria. Scientists call such an event a 'mass extinction' because it involves the extinction of so many different species.

The cause of dinosaur extinction

During the last million years of the existence of dinosaurs, the Earth underwent many dramatic changes, both in the climate and the environment. The temperature began to drop below zero for months and months and new mountain ranges began to form. Some seas became deeper and others dried up. Many species of plants became extinct because of the changes in the climate and new plants appeared with flowers. Perhaps the herbivore dinosaurs could not adapt to the new type of vegetation and began to die, so that there was no food for the carnivore dinosaurs. The decline of the dinosaur had already begun, at least for some groups. However, some fossilized remains have proved that at the end of the Cretaceous Period, some groups of dinosaurs were still managing to survive quite well. Therefore, something else must have happened, perhaps one single catastrophe..

The meteorite theory

There is evidence that, at the end of the Cretaceous Period, a meteorite weighing four million tonnes and with a diameter of ten kilometres, hit the Earth at a speed of nine thousand kilometres

Above: at the same time as dinosaurs existed, there were many species of other living things, such as the microscopic foraminifera. The Meteor Crater in Arizona, USA, is a huge crater made by the impact of a meteorite 45 metres in diameter. The Crater is 210 metres deep and measures over 1 kilometre in diameter.

an hour. The impact resulted in a terrible explosion, causing earthquakes, seaquakes and fires. Carbon dioxide and sulphur made the air toxic and a cloud of dust rose up; it blotted out the sun, so that plants could not make oxygen through the process of photosynthesis. This meant the temperature plummeted, resulting in acid rains and seas. At the same time there were powerful volcanic eruptions in India lasting millions of years and sending up great quantities of gas and ash into the air. Within a short time, almost all living things died: first the plants, then the herbivores, then the carnivores. When the dust settled and ceased to block out the light from the sun, the plants began to grow again – but the dinosaurs had gone.

Above: we know that 65 million years ago there were violent volcanic eruptions in India. They continued for millions of years, creating enormous devastation to the Earth and its environment.

Below: one of the most popular theories accepted by palaeontologists today is that a gigantic meteorite, 10 kilometres in diameter, hit the Earth 65 million years ago, causing the extinction of dinosaurs.

ALBERTOSAURUS

NAME: the name *Albertosaurus* comes from the place where its remains were first discovered: the province of Alberta, in Canada.

DISCOVERED BY: Osborne in 1905.

CLASSIFICATION: Saurischia, Theropoda, Tyrannosauridae.

REMAINS: Discovered in North America

DIMENSIONS: length: 8 metres
height: 3 metres
weight: 2 tonnes

FOOD: carnivore, that also ate dead or dying carcasses of other reptiles

CHARACTERISTICS: *Albertosaurus* was a biped with a huge head and powerful teeth. Its tiny little front limbs each ended in just two jointed digits. These limbs were too short to reach up to the dinosaur's mouth and yet they were very strong. So, what use were they? Experts have tried to establish what the function of these limbs could have been but so far they have not been able to answer this question.

Did you know that...

In 1996, the Canadian palaeontologist Philip Currie discovered some fossilized Albertosaurus skeletons all together! This exceptional find provided the first real evidence that these huge carnivore dinosaurs lived in herds. The question remains as to what disaster caused the death of all these dinosaurs at the same moment.

DINO QUIZ:

Dinosaurs of the *Tyrannosauridae* family, such as *Albertosaurus*, had a highly-jointed jaw. Why?

To widen the size of its bite.

The skull of an *Albertosaurus*.

NOW, AS THEN ...

it is probable that *Albertosaurus*, like all the large predators (hunting animals) today, as well as killing live prey, also fed on dead and dying carcasses.

ALLOSAURUS

NAME: *Allosaurus* means 'strange lizard'. The palaeontologist who discovered it thought that its bones were very similar to a lizard's.

DISCOVERED BY: Marsh in 1877.

CLASSIFICATION: Saurischia, Therapoda, Allosauridae.

REMAINS: *Allosaurus* remains have been found in North America, Europe, Africa, Australia, Asia and India.

DIMENSIONS: length: 14 metres
height: 5 metres
weight: 3 tonnes

FOOD: carnivore.

CHARACTERISTICS: The enormous quantity of remains in a good state of preservation has enabled palaeontologists to reconstruct the anatomy of the *Allosaurus* in fine detail. The *Allosaurus* was a powerful, agile animal, moving on two legs. Its skull was huge, its neck long and muscular. Its teeth curved inward and had jagged edges like a steak knife so as to cut through even the toughest skin. It would bite its prey, holding it firmly if it tried to escape. Its three-digit hands had strong, pointed claws, ideal for digging deep into its victim's flesh. It is thought that herds of *Allosaurus* could have hunted for prey as large as the gigantic *Camptosaurus* and *Stegosaurus*. The head of the *Allosaurus* had a strange bony crest which could have been used to recognize members of a herd, or to distinguish male from female.

Did you know that...

The Allosaurus could reach speeds of 30 kilometres an hour – with each leap measuring a good 3 metres! As it ran along, it kept its head down, its body parallel to the ground, with its tail, long and rigid, acting as a balance to keep the body stable.

Claws from the hand of *Allosaurus*: examples of various sizes.

DINO QUIZ:

The skull of an *Allosaurus* has two wide, deep holes. Can you guess what these were for?

A wide, round space enables the eyes to become well developed – and good eyesight is essential for successful hunting.

NOW, AS THEN ...

many experts believe that the *Allosaurus* had a hunting technique very similar to today's **tiger** – a long wait and then attacking at the shoulder of the prey, suddenly and rapidly.

ALVAREZSAURUS

NAME: means 'lizard of Alvarez' named after the historian Don Gregorio Alvarez.

DISCOVERED BY: Bonaparte in 1991.

CLASSIFICATION: Saurischia, Theropoda, Alvarezsauridae.

REMAINS: found in South America.

DIMENSIONS: length: 2 metres
height: 55 centimetres
weight: 8 kilograms

FOOD: carnivore, insectivore

CHARACTERISTICS: *Alvarezsaurus* was a biped dinosaur, agile and with a very light body, its feet and long rear limbs making it a fast runner. Its arms were very small and almost withered, so not much use. Its neck was 'S'-shaped and its stiff tail – more than a metre long – was used by the *Alvarezsaurus* to keep its balance.

Did you know that...

The Alvarezsaurus *is classified both among dinosaurs and within groups of primitive birds. The most recent discoveries seem to suggest that they are members of the dinosaur family – but there is still some disagreement about this.*

The *Alvarezsaurus* was a dinosaur closely linked to birds.

DINO QUIZ:

Why do palaeontologists believe that the *Alvarezsaurus* was a fast runner?

It had a slender, light skeleton, with long legs in relation to its body and the size of the bones of the legs.

NOW, AS THEN ...

the long 'S'-shaped neck of the *Alvarezsaurus* is like that of today's flightless birds, such as ostriches, emus and **rheas**.

ANATOTITAN
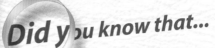

NAME: *Anatotitan* means 'gigantic duck'.

DISCOVERED BY: Chapman and Brett-Surman, 1990.

CLASSIFICATION: Ornithischia, Ornithopodopa, Hadrosauridae.

REMAINS: discovered in North America.

DIMENSIONS: length: 12 metres
height: 2.5 metres
weight: 5 tonnes

FOOD: herbivore.

CHARACTERISTICS: *Anatotitan* could walk very quickly on two legs but it normally ran on four legs. Its front legs were shorter than its strong hind legs and its feet ended with three digits each with a hoof. Its head was low and flat and with a wide, long beak. It had hundreds of teeth in its mouth which it used to grind up twigs and pines.

Did you know that...

Anatotitan *was originally named* Anatosaurus – *the duck reptile. Some experts think that, when attacked by a predator, it would flee into deep water. Its wide tail would have helped it to swim very rapidly.*

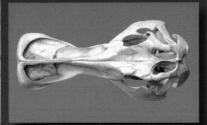

The skull of an *Anatotitan* seen from above.

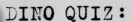

DINO QUIZ:

Experts have proof that the *Anatotitan* lived and moved from one place to another in herds. What makes them believe this?

The analysis of fossilized footprints and the direction of trails shows that large groups of hadrosaurs moved about together.

NOW, AS THEN ...

Anatotitan did not have a crest like other hadrosaurs. Instead it had two empty sacs at either side of its mouth which it may have been able to inflate – rather like those of the **elephant seal** today – in order to produce a loud, rumbling cry.

ANKYLOSAURUS

NAME: *Ankylosaurus* means 'stiff lizard'. Clearly this name was chosen due to the rigidity of the bony armour-plated covering.

DISCOVERED BY: Brown, 1908.

CLASSIFICATION: Ornithischia, Thyrephora, Anchylosauridae.

REMAINS: many fossilized remains of the *Ankylosaurus* have been found in North America – but no complete skeletons.

DIMENSIONS: length: 10 metres
height: 2.5 metres
weight: 4 tonnes.

FOOD: herbivore.

CHARACTERISTICS: *Ankylosaurus* was a massive, gigantic dinosaur, yet quite agile. It moved on four legs, keeping its front legs slightly bent sideways in order to support its weight better. Head, neck, back and tail were all protected by thick plates of solid bone, one overlapping the next to form one complete armour-plating from one side of the body to the other and with rows of strong, pointed spokes – an impenetrable defence against the teeth and the claws of the fiercest predators such as the *Albertosaurus* and the *Tyrannosaurus*. On its tail, the *Ankylosaurus* had a bony structure similar to a club – one powerful blow would be enough to break the bones of an enemy. Some scientists believe that this club was used not only as a means of defence but also in ritual fights between males in order to claim females during the mating season. The only part of the *Ankylosaurus* not covered by the armour-plating was the abdomen – and so it is possible that during attacks by more than one enemy, it would crouch down in order to protect this unprotected area of the body.

Did you know that...

Dinosaurs of the Ankylosaurus family died out at the end of the Cretaceous Period, between 65 and 68 million years ago. Therefore they were among the last dinosaurs to populate the Earth before the mass extinction.

DINO QUIZ:

Ankylosaurus had some bones in its skull and in its body fused together. Can you guess why?

Because this made the skeleton even stronger.

the armour-plating must have completely defended the adult *Ankylosaurus* against attack by predators – especially when combined with its extraordinary size – as daunting as that of today's huge elephant, the hippopotamus and the **rhinoceros**.

ANTONIO

NAME: this dinosaur was affectionately nicknamed 'Antonio' – but perhaps too hurriedly, because it now seems that the example found was female! It belongs to a newly-discovered species and its scientific name was given to it when the results of the first excavations were published.

DISCOVERED BY: Tiziana Brazzatti in 1995.

CLASSIFICATION: Ornithischia, Ornithopoda, Hadrosauridae.

REMAINS: discovered in Europe.

DIMENSIONS: length: 4 metres
height: 1.3 metres
weight: 700 kilograms.

FOOD: herbivore.

CHARACTERISTICS: *Antonio* was a biped dinosaur but it could also move on four legs. It fed on plant life which it minced up with rows of hundreds of teeth. It had a flat nose like a duck's beak and lived in herds with others of its type.

Did you know that...

Antonio *came to light in Trieste, at the Villaggio del Pescatore (Fishermen's Village) in the Duino area. It was the oldest and most complete example of a hadrosaur dinosaur to be found in the world, giving us important information as to how this group of dinosaurs developed and their possible area of origin.*

Past and Present

Up to about 15 years ago, it seemed impossible that any dinosaur fossils would be found in Italy. It was thought that, during the period when they lived, where the Italian peninsular is now there was a sea with lots of little islands – quite unsuitable for dinosaurs who were typically land-dwelling animals. But for some years now, remains of dinosaurs have begun to be discovered on Italian soil and earlier theories about the existence of Italy in the Mesozoic Era are being revised.

The island of Ponza, off the coast of Lazio.

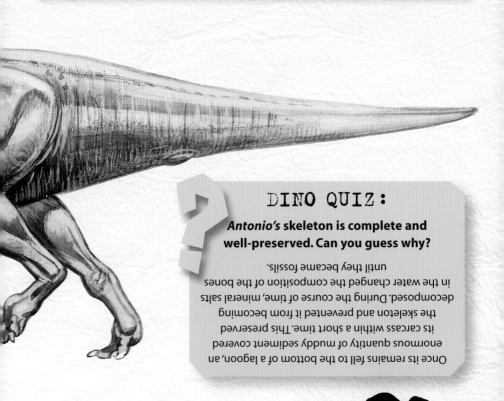

DINO QUIZ:

Antonio's skeleton is complete and well-preserved. Can you guess why?

Once its remains fell to the bottom of a lagoon, an enormous quantity of muddy sediment covered its carcass within a short time. This preserved the skeleton and prevented it from becoming decomposed. During the course of time, mineral salts in the water changed the composition of the bones until they became fossils.

APATOSAURUS

NAME: the name *Apatosaurus* means 'deceitful lizard'. In fact, this dinosaur 'deceived' Othniel Marsh, the palaeontologist who discovered it in 1877. He found some dinosaur bones and called it *Apatosaurus*. Two years later, he found other remains and, thinking that these belonged to another species, called the 'new' dinosaur *Brontosaurus* ('thunder lizard'). Only later was it found that all these bones belonged to the same species of dinosaur. The first name *Apatosaurus*, is actually the correct one.

DISCOVERED BY: Marsh in 1877.

CLASSIFICATION: Saurischia, Sauropoda, Diplodocidae.

REMAINS: the remains of the *Apatosaurus* were found in North America.

DIMENSIONS: length: 27 metres
height: 8 metres
weight: 35 tonnes.

FOOD: herbivore.

CHARACTERISTICS: *Apatosaurus* was a powerful dinosaur, characterized by legs like thick columns and a very long neck and tail – but with a head measuring only 55 centimetres, so tiny compared with the rest of the body! In its mouth it had long teeth at the front in the form of a sort of comb, useful for tearing leaves and shoots from branches of trees. The massive muscles in its back could have enabled the *Apatosaurus* to raise itself up on its hind legs to reach the most tender leaves at the tops of trees. The long tail, very thin at the end, was a formidable weapon which the *Apatosaurus* could swish from side to side at incredible speed, whistling like a whip and shattering the bones of any enemy trying to get near.

Did you know that...

During excavations one Apatosaurus skeleton and one Camarasaurus skeleton were unearthed – but only one skull. At that time, no complete skeletons had been found – but as the skull seemed to fit with the rest of the Apatosaurus remains, it was thought that the skull belonged to this dinosaur. For many years to come, the Apatosaurus was thought to have a skull which in fact, did not belong to it; only recently was it discovered that the skull belonged to the Camarasaurus! And so, the Apatosaurus lost its head and remained without one until the discovery of a new, complete skeleton with the 'right' skull ...

DINO QUIZ:

Apatosaurus, like many other sauropods, had hollow vertebrae. Can you guess why?

The dinosaur could be lighter, without losing strength.

NOW, AS THEN ...

defending by using the tail is not so unusual: the **iguana**, for example, behaves in the same way.

33

ARCHAEOPTERYX

NAME: *Archaeopteryx* means 'ancient wing'.

DISCOVERED BY: Meyer in 1861.

CLASSIFICATION: Bird, Archaeopterygidae.

REMAINS: found in Europe.

DIMENSIONS: length: 50 centimetres
height: 25 centimetres
weight: 50 grams.

FOOD: carnivore and insectivore.

CHARACTERISTICS: *Archaeopteryx* was a little like a small carnivore dinosaur and a little like a bird. Like all dinosaurs, it had a long tail, a sternum (the flat bone in the centre of the thorax), three strong clawed digits on each 'wing hand' and a mouth with lots of sharp teeth curving inward. As with all birds, the *Archaeopteryx* had a wishbone, two 'big toes' pointing backward for perching on branches of trees and a body covered with plumes and feathers. This makes the *Archaeopteryx* a classic link in evolution which demonstrates how birds have developed from dinosaurs. It is believed that the *Archaeopteryx* was a fine flyer.

Did you know that...

Archaeopteryx *is considered by many palaeontologists to be the oldest known bird. Study of the species has enabled scientists to understand the evolution of dinosaurs to birds and how they adapted to flight.*

DINO QUIZ:

What is a wishbone?

The wishbone is a small 'V'-shaped bone seen, for example, in the breast of a chicken. It is a bone which is curved as a result of the fusing of the two collar bones. It holds the muscles needed for the movement of the wings in flight.

The wishbone of a chicken.

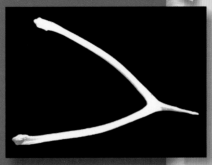

Past and Present

The discovery of the first example of *Archaeopteryx* in 1861 in Germany came at just the right time. Charles Darwin's 'theory of natural selection' was being discussed in the scientific world, dividing the 'evolutionists' and 'non-evolutionists'. The fossils of the *Archaeopteryx* made a great impact in this debate and supported Darwin's theory which he published for the first time under the title 'The Origin of the Species' in 1859.

ARGENTINOSAURUS

NAME: *Argentinosaurus* means 'Argentine lizard'.

DISCOVERED BY: Bonaparte and Coria, 1993.

CLASSIFICATION: Saurischia, Sauropoda, Titanosauridae.

REMAINS: found in South America.

DIMENSIONS: length: 40 metres
weight: 100 tonnes.

FOOD: herbivore.

CHARACTERISTICS: *Argentinosaurus* belongs to the family of land-dwelling animals which were probably the longest and heaviest which have ever existed. It was a gigantic dinosaur with an extremely long neck and tail, a somewhat slender body and tiny head; so, to excavate a complete skeleton of such a large dinosaur is very rare. For *Argentinosaurus*, for example, we have found only some sections – some vertebrae, fragments of ribs, one tibia and pelvic bones. The experience of the palaeontologists, their expert knowledge of anatomy of the giant plant-eating sauropods and the ratio of measurement between each section has enabled them to reconstruct their size and appearance.

Leg of an *Argentinosaurus*.

Did you know that...

Argentinosaurus *is a record-breaking animal. Its 100 tonne weight makes it the heaviest dinosaur known so far.*

DINO QUIZ:

What does 'sauropod' mean?

'Reptile feet'

NOW, AS THEN ...

the sauropod dinosaurs had huge pillar-like legs in order to support their enormous weight. The digits rested on flexible, soft pads like those of the **elephant**, the largest land-dwelling animal today.

BaGaCeRaTOPS

NAME: *Bagaceratops* means 'little-horned face'.

DISCOVERED BY: Maryanska and Halszaka Osmólska, in 1975.

CLASSIFICATION: Ornithischia, Marginocephalia, Protoceratopsidae.

REMAINS: found in Asia.

DIMENSIONS: length: 1 metre
height: 50 centimetres
weight: 22 kilograms

FOOD: herbivore.

CHARACTERISTICS: *Bagaceratops* was a quadruped dinosaur, small but powerful, with a distinctive, toothed, bony crest along the back edge of its skull and a small horn on its muzzle; it had strong jaws and teeth for finely chewing the vegetation on which it fed.

Did you know that...

Bagaceratops *is one of the dinosaurs which was found in Mongolia and it is regarded as one of the most primitive of the ceratopsians. As well as fossilized skeleton remains, its nests and eggs have been found.*

The skull of *Bagaceratops*.

NOW, AS THEN...

at the end of its mouth, *Bagaceratops* had a beak similar to that of a **parrot**, useful for cutting vegetation.

BARYONYX

NAME: *Baryonyx* means 'heavy claw' because it was the first example found of a fossilized hand with a claw.

DISCOVERED BY: Walker, in 1983.

CLASSIFICATION: Saurischi, Theropoda, Spinosauridae.

REMAINS: found in Europe.

DIMENSIONS: length: 10 metres
height: 4 metres
weight: 2 tonnes.

FOOD: piscivore.

CHARACTERISTICS: The skull of *Baryonyx* was very similar to that of a crocodile, narrow and elongated, with a very strong jaw and cone-shaped teeth. Between its eyes there was a bony crest. The front legs were long and strong, the hand having a thumb with a single curved claw. The rear legs were strong and erect, supporting the whole weight of the body which was balanced by a long tail, very broad at the base.

Did you know that...

It is very likely that *Baryonyx* lived in marshy areas and caught fish using its clawed thumb as a perfect hook for fishing. Among the fossilized bones of the rib cage of one example, numerous scales of a fish of the genus Lepidotes have been found; this was a very common fish in the Cretaceous period, almost a metre long. It is probable that these scales were the remains of the last meal of this Baryonyx.

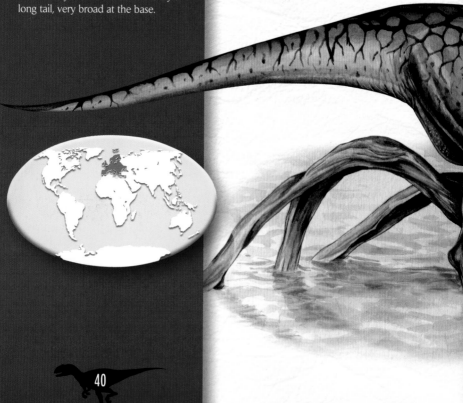

NOW, AS THEN ...

Baryonyx caught fish in the
same way as the **grizzly bear**
does in the rivers of North
America.

Some bones of the
rear leg of a
Baryonyx.

BeiPiaoSaurus

latest discovery

NAME: *Beipiaosaurus* means 'the lizard from Beipiao', the Chinese city near where it was found.

DISCOVERED BY: Xu, Tang and Wang, in 1999.

CLASSIFICATION: Saurischia, Theropoda, Therizinosauridae.

REMAINS: found in Asia.

DIMENSIONS: length: 2.20 metres
height: 90 centimetres
weight: 85 kilograms

FOOD: herbivore

CHARACTERISTICS: *Beipiaosaurus* had a beak without teeth and, further back in the mouth, two teeth which were used for chewing vegetation. It was a biped dinosaur with distinctive long claws on its hands. It was part of the family of therizinosaurid theropod dinosaurs which, unlike all the others of this group, probably fed on vegetal matter instead of meat.

Did you know that...

The fossil remains of an incomplete Beipiaosaurus discovered in Beipiao, in the province of Liaoning in China, have traces of fibres about 7 centimetres long on its skin: possibly they were primitive feathers which this dinosaur used, not for flying but to protect itself from the cold.

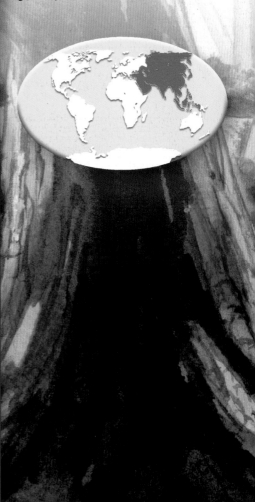

Some bones of the skeleton of *Beipiaosaurus*.

? DINO QUIZ:

What use are feathers to an animal which cannot fly?

Feathers are an excellent heat insulator and help a warm-blooded animal to keep its body temperature constant.

NOW, AS THEN...

the feather-like fibres of *Beipiaosaurus* would have looked like the fuzz which covers the head and neck of today's **ostriches**.

43

BOROGOVIA

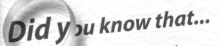

NAME: The strange name of *Borogovia* comes from the 'Borogoves', creatures looking like thin, scraggy birds with feathers sticking out all round like a mop, invented by Lewis Carroll. He described them in 'Through the Looking Glass', the sequel to 'Alice in Wonderland'.

DISCOVERED BY: Osmólska, in 1987.

CLASSIFICATION: Saurischia, Theropoda, Troodontidae.

REMAINS: discovered in Asia.

DIMENSIONS: length: 2 metres
height: 70 centimetres
weight: 13 kilograms.

FOOD: carnivore, perhaps omnivore.

CHARACTERISTICS: *Borogovia* was a small biped dinosaur, slender and capable of running very fast because of its exceptionally long hind legs; together with the other members of the family of troodontids, it belongs to the evolutionary line of the dromosaurids (which includes *Velociraptor*, for example) and of primitive birds.

Did you know that...

Like all troodontids, *Borogovia* had large eyes, for spotting small prey even in dim light and a very big brain, enabling it to hunt with cunning and skill.

When choosing the name of this dinosaur, the palaeontologist Osmólska was inspired by the Borogoves, characters in the story *Through the Looking Glass*.

NOW, AS THEN...

the most interesting characteristic of this animal is its cranial cavity, unusually large for a dinosaur, capable of containing a brain as well developed as those of **birds** today.

DINO QUIZ:

As well as being large, the eyes of *Borogovia* faced forward; why?

The frontal position of the eyes enabled it to perceive what it saw with the right eye and what it saw with the left as a single image; this was fundamental for it to hunt successfully because it enabled the distance of the prey to be estimated accurately.

BOTHRIOSPONDYLUS

NAME: *Bothriospondylus* means 'excavated vertebra'; this name was chosen because its vertebrae have large openings, the purpose of which was probably to make its long neck lighter.

DISCOVERED BY: Owen, in 1875.

CLASSIFICATION: Saurischia, Sauropoda, Brachiosauridae.

REMAINS: from Europe and Africa.

DIMENSIONS: length: 20 metres
height: 11 metres
weight: 35 tonnes.

FOOD: herbivore.

CHARACTERISTICS: *Bothriospondylus* was a quadruped dinosaur with a very long neck and front legs which were more developed than its hind legs. It was similar to the more famous *Brachiosaurus* but smaller.

Did you know that...

Bothriospondylus was one of the first dinosaurs discovered and it was described as long ago as 1876 by the English palaeontologist Richard Owen, who is credited with inventing the word 'dinosaur'. After Owen, no one was concerned with Bothriospondylus any more and a modern scientific description of this animal does not exist.

DINO QUIZ:

How do palaeontologists know what a dinosaur ate?

It is possible to make deductions from the teeth. For example, *Bothriospondylus* had long, spoon-shaped teeth adapted to feeding on the kind of leaves found at the tops of trees.

Past and Present

Bothriospondylus lived about 169 million years ago in the areas which now correspond to Britain, France and Madagascar.

The region of Mahajanga, Madagascar.

47

BRACHIOSAURUS

NAME: *Brachiosaurus* means 'dinosaur with arms'; the reason for this name lies in the fact that its front limbs were much longer than the hind ones, an extremely rare occurrence among vertebrates.

DISCOVERED BY: Riggs in 1903.

CLASSIFICATION: Saurischia, Sauropoda, Brachiosauridae.

REMAINS: found in Africa and North America.

DIMENSIONS: length: 25 metres
height: 13 metres
weight: 50 tonnes.

FOOD: herbivore.

CHARACTERISTICS: *Brachiosaurus* was a herbivore quadruped dinosaur with a very long neck. Unlike the other sauropods, it had front limbs which were much longer than the hind legs. It had teeth in the shape of a spatula, adapted to pulling leaves off the tops of trees. The first digit of the hand had a claw but the creature's best means of defence was to trample on predators which tried to come close to it.

Did you know that...

Brachiosaurus *was one of the largest animals ever to have trodden the Earth and it is one of the most famous and best known throughout the world. For decades the remains of* Brachiosaurus *were among the largest ever found. But it is no longer the largest dinosaur that has ever been seen: recently the remains of titanosaurians of even larger dimensions have been discovered.*

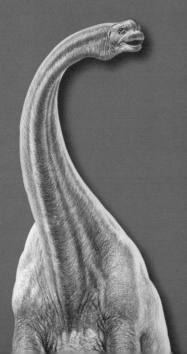

NOW, AS THEN...

The long neck and the fact that the front limbs were larger than the hind ones makes *Brachiosaurus* similar to a giant **giraffe**. This adaptation enabled it to feed off the tenderest shoots and leaves from the tops of trees.

49

CARCHARODONTOSAURUS

NAME: The name means 'lizard with shark's teeth' because the teeth of *Carcharodontosaurus* recall those of *Carcharodon*, the elasmobranch genus to which the great white shark belongs.

DISCOVERED BY: Stromer, in 1931.

CLASSIFICATION: Saurischia, Theropoda, Carcharodontosauridae.

REMAINS: found in North Africa.

DIMENSIONS: length: 14 metres
height: 4 metres
weight: 8 tonnes.

FOOD: carnivore, carrion eater.

CHARACTERISTICS: According to reconstructions by palaeontologists, *Carcharodontosaurus* was one of the largest carnivores ever to exist. Its body nonetheless looked elegant and slender, with a long tail, a strong neck, powerful hind limbs, well-developed front limbs and hands with three digits and sharp claws. The head was particularly impressive for its size (it was four times the size of a human!) and for its dozens of very sharp teeth, up to 12 centimetres long.

A *Carcharodontosaurus* tooth.

Did you know that...

Carcharodontosaurus came into the limelight in 1995 when the palaeontologist Paul Sereno and his team, working deep in the desert, discovered the remains of a new specimen: a complete half-skull, some vertebrae, parts of the limbs and the pelvis. It was a sensational discovery in that the head alone was almost 1 metre 70 centimetres long. This rivalled the skull of the largest Tyrannosaurus rex ever found.

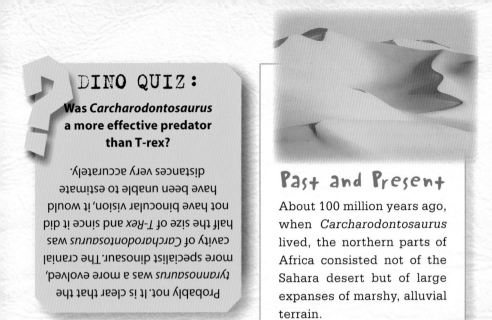

? DINO QUIZ:

Was *Carcharodontosaurus* a more effective predator than T-rex?

Probably not. It is clear that the *tyrannosaurus* was a more evolved, more specialist dinosaur. The cranial cavity of *Carcharodontosaurus* was half the size of *T-Rex* and since it did not have binocular vision, it would have been unable to estimate distances very accurately.

Past and Present

About 100 million years ago, when *Carcharodontosaurus* lived, the northern parts of Africa consisted not of the Sahara desert but of large expanses of marshy, alluvial terrain.

CARNOTAURUS

NAME: *Carnotaurus* means 'carnivorous bull'.

DISCOVERED BY: Bonaparte in 1985.

CLASSIFICATION: Saurischia, Theropoda, Abelisauridae.

REMAINS: from South America.

DIMENSIONS: length: 7.5 metres
height: 3 metres
weight: 1 tonne.

FOOD: carnivore.

CHARACTERISTICS: *Carnotaurus* was a large biped predator. The head was strong and imposing, with the teeth serrated like butcher's knives. The most distinctive features of this dinosaur were the two protuberances on its skull, like flat horns emerging above the eyes and its very short nose. Its arms were also unusual, very small in relation to the body, with a well-developed humerus but an extremely small radius and ulna. There were four digits on the hand, one of which, unusually, turned inwards. Scientists have not yet established what purpose the very small arms served, with the digits arranged in this unusual manner.

Did you know that...

The only remains of Carnotaurus were found in the prairies of Patagonia in Argentina in 1985. The palaeontologists were lucky enough also to find strips of fossilised skin, so they could form a more accurate idea of the external appearance of this creature. From the neck to the tail the skin had rows of small conical protuberances, while on the head were smaller little humps from which ran rows of large protuberant scales, covering the area round the eyes and the upper part of the nose.

NOW, AS THEN ...

Scholars believe that the male *Carnotaurus* had more developed horns than the female, like the **deer family** today.

DINO QUIZ:

Why are the teeth of many carnivorous animals curved towards the back?

To hold the prey firmly and to prevent it escaping easily from the predator's bite by struggling.

The Cave Bear also had notable defensive canine teeth which, being curved inwards, enabled it to rip the flesh of its enemies easily, by biting and tearing.

CERATOSAURUS

NAME: *Ceratosaurus* means 'horned reptile'.

DISCOVERED BY: O. C. Marsh in 1884.

CLASSIFICATION: Saurischia, Theropoda, Ceratosauridae.

REMAINS: found in North America and East Africa.

DIMENSIONS: length: 6 metres
height: 2 metres
weight: 900 kilograms.

FOOD: carnivore.

Did you know that...

The first remains of *Ceratosaurus* were found at the end of the 19th century but no complete skeletons exist. We know, however, that this dinosaur had some primitive characteristics —

CHARACTERISTICS: *Ceratosaurus* was a strange dinosaur distinguished by several little horns on its skull: a larger one on the nostrils and two smaller ones above the eyes. Its teeth were barbed and unusually large. Along the back and the tail was a kind of crest consisting of small, bony nodules. *Ceratosaurus* was a biped and the front limbs had hands with four digits.

for example the fourth digit in the hand. It is therefore thought that it was among the first great carnivorous dinosaurs to evolve, in response to the larger size of the herbivorous sauropods.

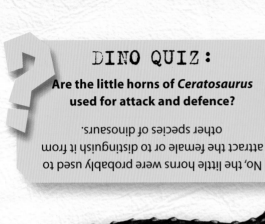

DINO QUIZ:

Are the little horns of *Ceratosaurus* used for attack and defence?

No, the little horns were probably used to attract the female or to distinguish it from other species of dinosaurs.

The skull of *Ceratosaurus* is distinctive with its little horns.

Past and Present

Ceratosaurus is a fascinating dinosaur and it has starred in many films. For example, in 'One Million Years B.C.', a film made in 1966, it was seen in battle with a *Triceratops* (even though *Triceratops* lived millions of years after *Ceratosaurus*!); it also made a brief appearance in 'Jurassic Park III' but it retreated quickly after it had scented the excrement of a terrible *Spinosaurus*.

COELOPHYSIS

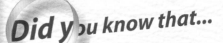

NAME: The name *Coelophysis* means 'hollow form': some of its bones have cavities which make the skeletal structure lighter.

DISCOVERED BY: Cope, in 1889.

CLASSIFICATION: Saurischia, Theropoda, Coelophysidae.

REMAINS: found in North America.

DIMENSIONS: length: 3 metres
height: 2 metres
weight: 27 kilograms.

FOOD: carnivore.

CHARACTERISTICS: *Coelophysis* was a dinosaur with a light, agile structure, adapted to speed. It moved quickly on two long, thin legs. The front limbs, about one-third of the length of the hind legs, terminated with four digits, three of them with claws. Small animals such as lizards, amphibians and insects were its commonest victims and *Coelophysis* easily captured them with the aid of its large eyes, long flexible neck and numerous small, sharp, serrated teeth. A herd of *Coelophysis* was also capable of killing larger prey. To preserve its balance during the complex manoeuvres of the hunt, *Coelophysis* used its tail which, stiffened by extension of the vertebrae, acted as a counterweight.

Did you know that...

Coelophysis was one of the first dinosaurs to appear in the Triassic era and it is among the most famous. In 1947, during an expedition in New Mexico in the United States, a group of researchers led by the palaeontologist Edwin Colbert made a sensational discovery. In the vicinity of Ghost Ranch, they brought to light hundreds of Coelophysis skeletons of various ages and sizes, laid down on top of each other. This was probably a herd which had died together – perhaps as a result of an unexpected, violent flood.

DINO QUIZ:

How do you know if a dinosaur is male or female?

It can be very difficult and even impossible to know whether a dinosaur is male or female. Nonetheless, intelligent guesses can be made. For example, there are two types of Coelophysis: one more heavily built and the other thinner. Palaeontologists believe that one category corresponds to the male and the other to the female but they do not know which is which.

NOW, AS THEN ...

in the chest cavity of some *Coelophysis* adults, remains of little animals of the same species have been found. At first scientists thought that these were young animals not yet born but dinosaurs lay eggs and do not give birth to their young; also these creatures were already too large to have been in an egg. The most likely hypothesis is therefore that the adults, for whatever reason, devoured some little ones of the same species. Even today some mammals do this: **cats**, for example, eat their own kittens when they are born with some abnormality.

COMPSOGNATHUS

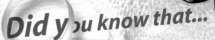

NAME: *Compsognathus* means 'elegant jaw'.

DISCOVERED BY: Wagner, in 1859.

CLASSIFICATION: Saurischia, Theropoda, Compsognathidae.

REMAINS: found in Europe.

DIMENSIONS: length: 1 metre
weight: 3 kilograms.

FOOD: carnivore.

CHARACTERISTICS: *Compsognathus* was a small, nimble dinosaur with a long, flexible neck, thin, energetic limbs and large eyes for spotting and catching small prey. It had front limbs with, unusually, only two digits and a long tail which was useful for keeping it stable when it was running. The skull was small and elongated while the mouth contained many very sharp teeth.

Did you know that...

Compsognathus *is famous for its small size, although even smaller dinosaurs are known. We know with certainty what it ate because, inside the stomach of an example found in Germany the fossilized skeleton of a small lizard of the genus* Bavarisaurus *is visible. To catch these very fast-moving animals,* Compsognathus *must have been a very agile runner.*

NOW, AS THEN ...

Compsognathus was comparable in size to a **chicken** – but one with a very long tail.

DINO QUIZ:

How do we know how fast a dinosaur could run?

In 1976 the American zoologist R. McNeil Alexander formulated an equation which gives the speed that an animal can achieve when running: **velocity** (m/s) = $\mathbf{0.25 \times g^{0.5} \times SL^{1.67} \times h^{-1.17}}$ in which **g** is standard gravity, 9.8 m/sec², **SL** is the length of stride of the animal being measured, which in the case of a dinosaur can be taken from footmarks in fossils and **h** is the height of the limb from the ground to the pelvis.

CORYTHOSAURUS

NAME: *Corythosaurus* means 'helmeted lizard', after the shape of the crest on top of its skull.

DISCOVERED BY: Brawn, in 1914.

CLASSIFICATION: Ornithischia, Ornithopoda, Hadrosauridae.

REMAINS: found in North America.

DIMENSIONS: length: 10 metres
weight: 5 tonnes.

FOOD: herbivore.

CHARACTERISTICS: *Corythosaurus* is part of the group of dinosaurs known as 'duck-beaked' which are distinguished by a long, flat skull ending in a sharp, horny beak. At the front, the muzzle was gap-toothed but in the rear part of the mouth there were hundreds of teeth, arranged in several rows, for efficiently chewing the vegetation on which the animal fed; this included small branches, roots, pine cones and seeds. *Corythosaurus* could move on all fours or on two legs; it had arms shorter than the legs and a long tail which balanced it as it moved. It did not have armour, quills or claws but could avoid dangerous predators because of its excellent sight and good sense of hearing; in perilous situations it relied on taking flight rapidly.

Did you know that...

Corythosaurus had a particular crest on its skull, the tall, narrow shape of which recalls that of an ancient Greek helmet. The crest was hollow inside and connected to the airways of the nose and mouth. It is thought that the crest was used by the animal as a resonating chamber so that it could emit loud sounds, characteristic cries which would enable individuals of the same species to recognise each other or to warn the herd in case of danger. Another theory suggests that the crest was used to improve the capacity of its sense of smell so that it could detect the scent of an approaching predator. It seems that the males had more developed crests than the females and the young of the herd.

NOW, AS THEN ...

some experts say that *Corythosaurus* was able to plunge into the waters of a river or a lake like an enormous **duck** and to swim towards the opposite bank in order to save itself from attack by predators.

CRYOLOPHOSAURUS

NAME: *Cryolophosaurus* means 'frozen crested lizard', from the distinctive crest on its head and from the fact that it comes from the frozen continent of Antarctica.

DISCOVERED BY: Hammer and Hickerson, in 1994.

CLASSIFICATION: Saurischia, Theropoda, Ceratosauria.

REMAINS: found in Antarctica.

DIMENSIONS: length: 6 metres
height: 1 metre
weight: 525 kilograms

FOOD: carnivore.

CHARACTERISTICS: *Cryolophosaurus* was a biped dinosaur of remarkable size with a large skull and a prominent crest. Because the shape of the crest is reminiscent of the 1960s quiff of the singer Elvis Presley, *Cryolophosaurus* has been nicknamed 'Elvisaurus'.

Did you know that...

The Cryolophosaurus is an important dinosaur because it is the first to have been found in the Antarctic. Unlike other parts of the world, very few dinosaur fossils have been discovered in the continent of Antarctica.

The singer Elvis Presley.

DINO QUIZ:

Why was Antarctica close to the equator in the Jurassic period and not in the same position as it is today?

According to the geological theory of continental drift, the continents are very slowly but continuously moving in relation to each other, driven by the movements and convection currents within the Earth's semi-liquid and very hot mantle layer which is beneath the Earth's crust.

Past and Present

An iceberg in the Antarctic.

In the Jurassic period, when Cryolophosaurus lived, the Antarctic was a much warmer environment than it is today; it was actually quite close to the equator.

DaCenTRURUS

NAME: The name means 'spiky tale' because *Dacentrurus* had long, sharp-pointed spikes along its tail.

DISCOVERED BY: Owen, in 1875.

CLASSIFICATION: Ornithischia, Thyreophora, Stegosauridae.

REMAINS: discovered in Europe.

DIMENSIONS: length: 5 metres
height: 1.80 metres
weight: 3 tonnes.

FOOD: herbivore.

CHARACTERISTICS: *Dacentrurus* moved slowly and heavily on its four legs. Its head was very small in proportion to the volume of its body and its short teeth were used for chewing softer vegetation. It had a crested crown, sharp-pointed plates along its spine and tail and some very vicious spikes on its tail. If a predator dared to attack *Dacentrurus* from behind, a few blows of its tail would have wounded it and put it to flight.

Did you know that...

Dacentrurus *was a fairly primitive stegosaur. Partial remains found in France suggest that it could reach a length of 10 metres: if this should be the case, it would be one of the largest stegosaurs.*

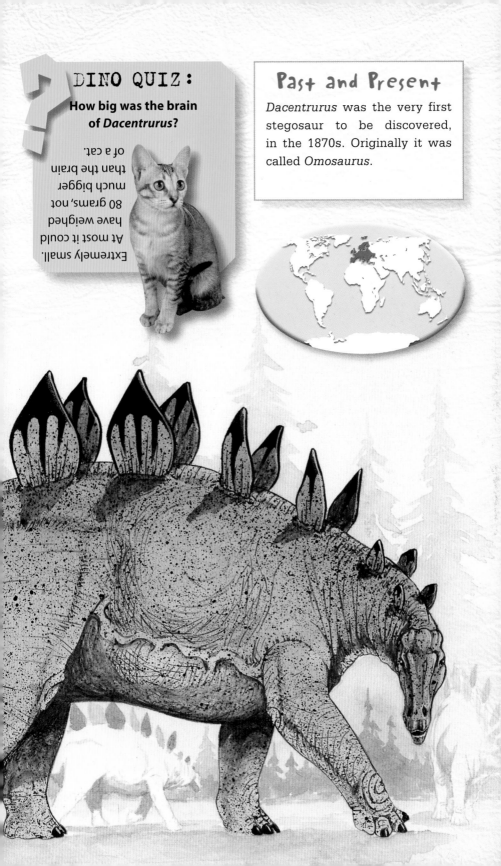

DINO QUIZ:

How big was the brain of *Dacentrurus*?

Extremely small. At most it could have weighed 80 grams, not much bigger than the brain of a cat.

Past and Present

Dacentrurus was the very first stegosaur to be discovered, in the 1870s. Originally it was called *Omosaurus*.

DEINOCHEIRUS

NAME: The name means 'terrible hand', probably because *Deinocheirus* had highly developed, very strong hands and claws.

DISCOVERED BY: Osmólska and Roniewicz, in 1970.

CLASSIFICATION: Saurischia, Theropoda, Deinocheiridae.

REMAINS: discovered in Asia.

DIMENSIONS: There is not enough data to enable the size of this dinosaur to be reliably estimated.

FOOD: not known.

CHARACTERISTICS: The only thing that is certain about *Deinocheirus* is that its hands ended with very strong fingers, curved and pointed; everything else is hypothetical. Some palaeontologists believe that *Deinocheirus* resembles *Therizinosaurus*, a strange dinosaur with highly developed forelegs; other scholars believe that *Deinocheirus* has more in common with the ornithomimids, fast runners with long legs; yet others believe it is akin to *Deinonychus*.

The large forelegs of *Deinocheirus*.

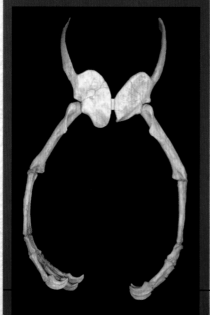

Did you know that...

The only fossils of *Deinocheirus* that have so far been found are the front parts: two enormous limbs which measure 2.50 metres from the end of the humerus to the point of the claws!

NOW, AS THEN ...

The arms, hands and claws of *Deinocheirus* have no equivalent in nature today.

DINO QUIZ:

What could the enormous claws of *Deinocheirus* have been used for?

Several possibilities have been suggested, such as ripping open the bellies of their victims, hanging from large trees, or digging in search of food.

Deinonychus

NAME: The name *Deinonychus* means 'terrible claw'.

DISCOVERED BY: Ostrom, in 1969.

CLASSIFICATION: Saurischia, Theropoda, Dromeosauridae.

REMAINS: Found in North America.

DIMENSIONS: length: 3.5 metres
height: 2 metres
weight: 70 kilograms.

FOOD: carnivore.

CHARACTERISTICS: *Deinonychus* was one of the most dangerous predators of the Cretaceous period. It was an extremely agile and effective hunter, capable of clustering together in herds, planning a strategy of attack and knocking down larger animals. It had long legs and a rigid back to counterbalance its body weight, barbed teeth and formidable claws on its hind legs. The most terrible weapon of this dinosaur was on the second digit of each foot: a large, sharp curved claw, in the form of a crescent. While walking or running this claw was retracted, so that it did not touch the soil but when the animal launched a kick and the foot was extended, a tendon pulled it forward, so that it was released like a blade from a penknife. Its long, jointed arms and the ability to rotate its wrists, enabled *Deinonychus* to hold on to its prey. The hind legs were used for kicking while the sickle-like claws ripped open the victim.

Did you know that...

Deinonychus is a very significant dinosaur scientifically because its discovery in 1969 by the American palaeontologist John Ostrom has contributed decisively to the formulation of a theory that there were warm-blooded dinosaurs, able to regulate their body temperature by internal biological methods. So it is likely that Deinonychus had a skin covered with some kind of plumage.

NOW, AS THEN ...

The dromoaeosaurs, such as _Deinonychus_, were capable of coordinating themselves to hunt large predators as a pack. For instance, bones of a group of _Deinonychus_ have been brought to light surrounding the skeleton of a herbivorous dinosaur, 6 metres long, of the genus _Tenontosaurus_. Many carnivores of the present day, such as **wolves** or lions, use the same hunting tactic.

DILOPHOSAURUS

NAME: *Dilophosaurus* means 'two-crested lizard'. It is so-named because it has two tall crests on its head.

DISCOVERED BY: Welles, in 1970.

CLASSIFICATION: Saurischia, Theropoda, Ceratosauridae.

REMAINS found in North America.

DIMENSIONS: length: 7 metres
weight: 400 kilograms.

FOOD: carnivore.

CHARACTERISTICS: *Dilophosaurus* had a strange head: the muzzle was long and on the top of its head were two tall, bony crests, thin, curved and positioned in such a way as to form a kind of 'V'. Its teeth were like curved, serrated hooks. It walked as a biped and was an excellent predator, agile and fast.

Did you know that...

Dilophosaurus *lived at the start of the Jurassic period, about 190 million years ago and it was one of the first large-sized carnivorous dinosaurs. Its primitiveness was demonstrated by the presence of four digits on each hand, although the fourth digit was very reduced (in the course of evolution, there is a noticeable tendency for carnivorous dinosaurs to have fewer digits on the hand).*

Dilophosaurus had a twin crest forming a 'V' on its head.

DINO QUIZ:

Is it true that *Dilophosaurus* spat venom in the face of its victims?

There is no scientific evidence to support this hypothesis.

NOW, AS THEN ...

The delicate and fleshy, crest of a **cock**, has no defensive function, nor is it used as a weapon but with its garish shape and colour, it is ornamental and attracts the female of the same species. Perhaps the twin crest of *Dilophosaurus* had a similar purpose.

DIPLODOCUS

NAME: The name *Diplodocus* means 'double beam', a reference to the particular bone structure of its back, which is reminiscent of the supporting framework of a suspension bridge.

DISCOVERED BY: O. C. Marsh, in 1878.

CLASSIFICATION: Saurischia, Sauropoda, Diplodocidae.

REMAINS: found in North America.

DIMENSIONS: length: up to 50 metres
height: 6 metres
weight: 30 tonnes.

FOOD: herbivore.

CHARACTERISTICS: This was a dinosaur with an enormous body, a long tail held horizontally and a tiny skull, so small that a similarly-proportioned human being would have a head a quarter of a centimetre in diameter! It had pencil-shaped teeth only in the front part of its mouth, used like a rake to gather the leaves of bushes and plants. The tail, very long with a soft part at the end, was a terrible weapon: operated by powerful muscles, it swung from side to side at incredible speed, making a whistling noise like a whip. It could smash the legs of unwary predators which approached the herd. It moved slowly on its four column-like legs, grazing on the wide expanses of the Jurassic plains.

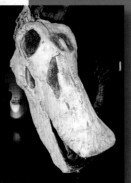

Diplodocus had a small skull with a long flat muzzle.

Did you know that...

Diplodocus *holds a record: it is the longest dinosaur known in the world. In New Mexico fossils of an example of it have been found with a length of 50 metres! It was however a relatively 'light' animal in terms of mass, weighing no more than 30 tonnes.*

DINO QUIZ:

Why was *Diplodocus* so big?

The enormous increase in size was probably due to natural selection of specimens which, being bigger, managed to defend themselves against carnivores, thus ensuring their survival.

NOW, AS THEN ...

Today no land animals are as big as the sauropod dinosaurs were. The largest creature existing today is the **blue whale**, 30 metres long and weighing 200 tons but this is an animal which lives in water, an environment where supporting such a weight is much less difficult than on land.

DROMICEIOMIMUS

NAME: The name *Dromiceiomimus* means 'emu look-alike'.

DISCOVERED BY: Russell, in 1972.

CLASSIFICATION: Saurischia, Theropoda, Ornitomimidae.

REMAINS: found in North America.

DIMENSIONS: length: 3.5 metres
weight: 150 kilograms

FOOD: omnivore.

CHARACTERISTICS: This dinosaur, like the Australian emu of today, had a fairly short body, supported by long, strong hind legs. It had a soft, elongated neck and a small head with no teeth but with large eyes, perhaps to see and hunt better during the night. Unlike the emu, it had a long tail and well-developed arms with claws, enabling it to grasp its food and prey easily.

Did you know that...

Dromiceiomimus *very much resembles an emu and it was a very fast-moving animal; it survived by using its large eyes to spot potential predators easily – and then running away.*

DINO QUIZ:

What speed could running dinosaurs such as *Dromiceiomimus* reach?

Ornithomimids, (running dinosaurs), could probably reach a speed of about 55 kilometres per hour.

NOW, AS THEN ...

The skull of *Dromiceiomimus* was as large and developed as that of an **emu** living in the present day.

EDMONTONIA

NAME: The name *Edmontonia* was chosen to record the area where it was discovered: the Edmonton rock formation in Alberta, Canada.

DISCOVERED BY: Sternberg, in 1928.

CLASSIFICATION: Ornithischia, Thyreophora, Nodosauridae.

REMAINS: found in North America.

DIMENSIONS: length: 7 metres
height: 1.6 metres
weight: 3.5 tonnes

FOOD: herbivore.

CHARACTERISTICS: *Edmontonia* was a strong, ponderous dinosaur which moved slowly on its four dumpy legs. Its body was covered with plates and it had bony protuberances on its back and flanks. On the sides of the body was a row of very prominent bony spikes. The long, flattened skull was also surrounded by strong sheets of protective bone; the teeth were fairly small and the jaws were slight but with a sharp beak which was useful for cutting vegetation.

Did you know that...

Unlike other armoured dinosaurs, Edmontonia did not have a club on its tail. Its only defences were the hard armour in which it was clad and the long bony spikes it had on both shoulders.

The teeth of *Edmontonia* were small with a surface adapted to chewing plants.

DINO QUIZ:

What is a significant difference between a nodosaurid, such as *Edmontonia* and other armoured dinosaurs of the family of ankylosaurs?

The nodosaurids do not have a club on their tail like ankylosaurs.

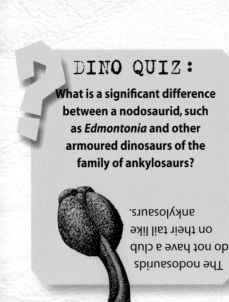

NOW, AS THEN ...

When it was attacked, *Edmontonia* probably squatted on the ground to present its hard armour to the predator and to protect its stomach. **Armadillos** today, also protected by armour, squat when they are attacked and can roll themselves up like a ball to protect the abdomen.

eoraptor

NAME: *Eoraptor* was a very primitive dinosaur and for this reason it has been given the name 'dawn hunter'.

DISCOVERED BY: Sereno, Forster, Rogers, Monetta, in 1993.

CLASSIFICATION: Saurischia, Theropoda.

REMAINS: found in South America.

DIMENSIONS: length: 1 metre
weight: 10 kilograms.

FOOD: carnivore.

CHARACTERISTICS: *Eoraptor* walked on two hind legs and was very agile and fairly speedy. Its arms were about half the length of the legs and had five digits; the three longest digits ended with large claws, useful for catching and holding prey, which probably consisted of small animals such as insects and lizards.

Did you know that...

Eoraptor *is one of the most primitive dinosaurs known. It was agile and quick and lived at the end of the Triassic period.*

Past and Present

The fossil remains of *Eoraptor* come from Argentina, specifically the formation called the **'Ischigualasto Basin'**.
In the late Triassic, this region was not a desert zone as it is today but a valley through which rivers ran.

DINO QUIZ:

What characteristics indicate that *Eraptor* was a primitive dinosaur?

Eoraptor's hand was very primitive because it had five digits. Also some of its teeth were those of a carnivore and others were similar to those of primitive herbivores. It is therefore thought that *Eoraptor* was a forebear of the prosauropods, the dinosaurs which were the precursors of the gigantic herbivores with long necks.

The skull of *Eoraptor*.

79

EOTYRannus

NAME: *Eotyrannus* means 'dawn tyrant'

DISCOVERED BY: Hutt, Naish, Martill, Barker, Newberry, in 2001.

CLASSIFICATION: Saurischia, Theropoda, Tyrannosauroidea.

REMAINS: found in Europe.

DIMENSIONS: length: 6 metres

FOOD: carnivore.

CHARACTERISTICS: *Eotyrannus* was a primitive tyrannosaur, because it did not have the characteristic large brain nor the front legs reduced to stumps in its celebrated relative, tyrannosaurus; it was an animal with a fairly small skull and light constitution, with long front legs that had three digits. It hunted its prey with agility and it is possible that, like other primitive tyrannosaurs (for instance, the Chinese example belonging to the genus Dilong), it had a fibrous covering like primitive feathers.

Did you know that...

Eotyrannus *came from the Isle of Wight, an island situated off the southern coast of England and it is a possible forebear of the celebrated Tyrannosaurus rex. Palaeontologists think that this recent discovery is the missing link in the evolutionary history of Tyrannosaurus rex, which lived between 60 and 70 million years ago, when the skeleton of Eotyrannus was already 55 million years old!*

Past and present

The presence of a dinosaur from the tyrannosaurus family, typical of the American continent, in England, has supported the suggestion that during the Cretaceous period the British **Isle of Wight** was part of the eastern coast of North America.

DINO QUIZ:

What dinosaurs did *Eotyrannus* hunt?

Eotyrannus probably hunted dinosaurs such as *Hypsilophodon* and *Iguanodon*, remains of which came from the same region and rocks of the same period.

81

EUPLOCEPHALUS

NAME: *Euplocephalus* means 'well-armed head'.

DISCOVERED BY: Lambe, in 1910.

CLASSIFICATION: Ornithischia, Thyreophora, Ankylosauridae.

REMAINS: found in North America.

DIMENSIONS: length: 7 metres
weight: 2.5 tonnes

FOOD: herbivore.

CHARACTERISTICS: *Euplocephalus* was a quadruped dinosaur, slow and ponderous. The upper part of its body, including its neck and head, were covered with large bony plates, which formed a continuous coat of armour, with cone-shaped projections. This armour was a useful protection against enemy attacks.

Did you know that...

Euplocephalus *was a herbivorous armoured dinosaur, related to the better-known Anchilosaurus. It used the powerful club on its tail to defend itself against very dangerous predators such as the tyrannosaurs, its contemporaries.*

DINO QUIZ:

How did *Euplocephalus* move its heavy tail with accuracy and hit predators with its club?

Euplocephalus had a strong muscle between the leg and tail, called the caudal femur, which was used to move its heavy weapon.

past and present

Euplocephalus moved at a maximum speed of 7 kilometres per hour, about the same as a **human** walking at a sustained pace.

FABROSAURUS

NAME: *Fabrosaurus* was named 'Fabre lizard' by the palaeontologist Leonard Ginsburg in honour of Jean Henri Fabre, a famous French entymologist who wrote about insects.

DISCOVERED BY: Ginsburg, in 1964.

CLASSIFICATION: Ornithischia, Ornithopoda.

REMAINS: Found in South Africa.

DIMENSIONS: length: 1 metre

FOOD: herbivore.

CHARACTERISTICS: *Fabrosaurus* was a dinosaur of small size which probably moved in biped posture, had arms shorter than its legs and fed on plants. Its teeth were small, set in its fairly long jaws and it may have had a horny beak for cutting vegetation.

Did you know that...

Fabrosaurus was a primitive dinosaur. Its remains were found in Lesotho, a region of South Africa, where it lived between the end of the Triassic and start of the Jurassic periods, about 200 million years ago.

DINO QUIZ:

Why do palaeontologists know so little about *Fabrosaurus*?

Very little is known about this dinosaur because the only remains consist of a fragment of the jawbone with a few teeth.

Fabrosaurus had small teeth with serrated edges like leaves.

84

past and present

Often palaeontologists have problems when they have to classify and reconstruct the appearance of an animal which lived millions and millions of years ago. The scientific classification of *Fabrosaurus* is very uncertain; according to some scholars it may not even have existed, because the remains resemble a dinosaur of the genus *Lesothosaurus*, found in the same region.

Marakabei region of Lesotho.

FULGUROTHERIUM

NAME: *Fulgurotherium* means 'beast of lightning', a name taken from that of the area where it was found, Lightning Ridge.

DISCOVERED BY: Huene, in 1932.

CLASSIFICATION: Ornithischia, Ornithopoda, Hypsilophodontidae.

REMAINS: found in Australia.

DIMENSIONS: length: 2 metres

FOOD: herbivore.

CHARACTERISTICS: *Fulgurotherium* was a small, light, herbivorous dinosaur with sharp sight and a well-developed sense of hearing. It had a sharp beak and moved with long strides and big leaps on agile limbs. It is very likely that it lived in herds.

The opal is a mineral which exists in many varieties of colour. It is used to make precious objects and jewellery. One of the largest deposits of opals is to be found in Australia.

Did you know that...

Fulgurotherium *lived in Australian forests and plains crossed by numerous water courses, about 110 million years ago. Palaeontologists have only the bones of its legs and one of its shoulder blades. These few remains are still remarkable because they were opalised during the process of fossilisation. The calcium phosphate of the bone was replaced by opal, a rare, precious mineral, with colours varying from transparent to milk white and mottled with beautiful green, red, yellow, brown or even black reflections.*

DINO QUIZ:

Why did many herbivorous dinosaurs, such as *Fulgurotherium*, live in herds?

Living in a herd was a great advantage for herbivorous dinosaurs; while some were grazing peacefully, others could mount guard, watching every movement very carefully and giving warning if a carnivore was approaching.

Past and Present

In the Cretaceous period, when *Fulgurotherium* lived, part of Australia was connected to the **Antarctic**. Scholars believe that each winter herds of *Fulgurotherium* migrated to the north to avoid the cold of the polar region.

87

GALLIMIMUS

NAME: *Gallimimus* means 'chicken mimic'.

DISCOVERED BY: Barsbold, Osmólska and Roniewicz, in 1972.

CLASSIFICATION: Saurischia, Theropoda, Ornithomimidae.

REMAINS: found in Mongolia.

DIMENSIONS: length: 4 metres
height: 2 metres
weight: 440 kilograms

FOOD: omnivore.

CHARACTERISTICS: *Gallimimus* was a fast-running dinosaur with a small body and long, thin legs. It had a long, S-shaped neck, a small head, large eyes, a well-developed ridged beak and short, powerful arms with three digits. It ate plants, small animals including insects and lizards and perhaps even eggs.

Did you know that...

Speed and a well-developed brain were the best assets of the Gallimimus in its daily struggle to survive. It shared these characteristics with the other dinosaurs of the ornithomimosaurid family to which it belongs.

DINO QUIZ:

What is an omnivore?

An omnivore is a creature which can eat both vegetables and animals; its digestive system is able to assimilate cellulose, the fibres of which are found in both plant and animal proteins.

The skull of a *Gallimimus*.

NOW, AS THEN ...

Gallimimus had a lifestyle which very much resembled that of the large, fast-running birds of today: the African ostrich, the Australian **emu** and the American rhea.

GIGANOTOSAURUS

NAME: *Giganotosaurus* means 'giant lizard of the south'. In particular, the 'notos' part of its name refers to the south winds.

DISCOVERED BY: Coria and Salgano, in 1995.

CLASSIFICATION: Saurischia, Theropoda, Carcharodontosauridae.

REMAINS: discovered in South America.

DIMENSIONS: length: 14.5 metres
weight: 8 tonnes

FOOD: carnivore.

CHARACTERISTICS: *Giganotosaurus* was a biped and used its long, rigid tail like a balancing pole to maintain its equilibrium. Its skull was about 1.80 metres long and it must have seemed enormous and terrifying.
Its huge jaws and sharp, pointed teeth enabled it to tear a large chunk of flesh from the body of its prey in a single bite. It is probable that they lived in groups because palaeontologists have discovered several *Giganotosaurus* fossil skeletons next to each other.
We also know its favourite food: near the site where *Giganotosaurus* was discovered, fossil remains of *Argentinosaurus* were also found, suggesting to scientists that this carnivore had preyed upon these enormous herbivores.

Did you know that...

Giganotosaurus was among the largest predators that ever lived on Earth and with its length of 14.5 metres it holds the record as the longest carnivorous dinosaur. This puts the supremacy of Tyrannosaurus rex in doubt, because Giganotosaurus was a longer dinosaur; however, it must have been thinner and therefore lighter.

past and present

The remains of *Giganotosaurus* were discovered in **Argentina** in a place very popular with palaeontologists because it is here that the largest dinosaurs have been discovered.

DINO QUIZ:

Where are the remains of Giganotosaurus kept?

The original fossils of Giganotosaurus are on display at the Carmen Funes Municipal Museum in Neuquén province in Argentina.

91

GILMOREOSAURUS

NAME: *Gilmoreosaurus* means 'Gilmore's lizard', in honour of Gilmore, the scientist who described it but erroneously attributed it to the *Manchurosaurus* genus.

DISCOVERED BY: Brett-Surman, in 1979.

CLASSIFICATION: Ornithischia, Ornithopoda.

REMAINS: discovered in Asia.

DIMENSIONS length: 8 metres
weight: 2 tonnes

FOOD: herbivore.

CHARACTERISTICS: *Gilmoreosaurus* was a dinosaur with a duck-billed beak, able to move on either two or on four legs and with claw-like toes to help it run. It probably spent most of the day on four legs, browsing among the vegetation which it tore with its beak and chewed with its numerous back teeth. The females of the herd built circular nests on the ground.

Did you know that...

Gilmoreosaurus is known mainly through the discovery of some fossil teeth and a few bones. This is why palaeontologists are not sure about its classification; many believe that it was a primitive hadrosaur but others think that it belongs to the group of iguanodons.

DINO QUIZ:

How did _Gilmoreosaurus_ defend itself against predators?

Gilmoreosaurus lived in a herd. A herd is more effective than a single individual in sighting a predator in time, thus enabling its members to flee and rapidly escape.

past and present

Palaeontologists have formed an accurate idea of what _Gilmoreosaurus_ looked like on the basis of the few remains discovered. This is possible because every bone has a particular shape for carrying out a specific function and can therefore tell us much about the body from which it comes.

GIRAFFATITAN

NAME: *Giraffatitan* means 'titanic giraffe', based on its resemblance to a giant giraffe.

DISCOVERED BY: Paul, in 1988.

CLASSIFICATION: Saurischia, Sauropoda, Brachiosauridae.

REMAINS: discovered in Central Africa.

DIMENSIONS: length: 23 metres
height: 12 metres
weight: 50 tonnes.

FOOD: herbivore.

CHARACTERISTICS: The distinctive feature of *Giraffatitan* was its skull: at the top of its head it had a prominent nasal crest and its mouth was rounded. Apart from this it was quite similar to *Brachiosaurus*. *Giraffatitan* moved very slowly and heavily on its four column-like legs.

Did you know that...

Giraffatitan *was a dinosaur very similar to the famous* Brachiosaurus: *extremely large with a very long neck, tiny head and front legs longer than the back legs, giving it a typical 'giraffe' look.*

DINO QUIZ:

How many vertebrae does the very long neck of *Giraffatitan* have?

There are only a dozen cervical vertebrae in the neck of sauropod dinosaurs. Each vertebra is therefore several tens of centimetres long.

NOW, AS THEN ...

The 'leaning' appearance of *Giraffatitan* is reminiscent of that of the **giraffe** of today. It too ate leaves, twigs and the more tender branches at the top of tall trees.

GOYOCEPHALE

NAME: *Goyocephale*, the dinosaur with the 'decorated head', was so named because of the bony spikes at the top of its skull.

DISCOVERED BY: Perle, Maryanska and Osmolska, in 1982.

CLASSIFICATION: Ornithischia, Marginocephalia, Pachycephalosauridae.

REMAINS: discovered in Asia.

DIMENSIONS: length: 2 metres
weight: 10-40 kilograms

FOOD: herbivore.

CHARACTERISTICS: *Goyocephale* was a biped and fed on plants. The bony dome on top of its skull was a weapon displayed during fights between males but it was also a useful defence against other dinosaurs.
When *Goyocephale* was ready to attack it lowered its head and, with its spine parallel to the ground, took a run and violently head-butted its opponent.

Did you know that...

Goyocephale *was a dinosaur with a kind of protective 'helmet' on its head: the bones of its skull were extremely thick and had spiky growths on top.*

? DINO QUIZ:

How thick was the skull of *Goyocephale*?

The thickest part of the protective bony layer of *Goyocephale*'s skull was 20 centimetres thick or more.

NOW, AS THEN ...

Perhaps the *Goyocephale* used its helmeted head as a weapon when fighting other males of the same species during the mating season, as **mouflons** and **wild goats** still do today.

HaDROSaURUS

NAME: *Hadrosaurus* means 'stout lizard' and it has given its name to the duck-billed family of dinosaurs, a group of ornithopods descended from the iguanodonts.

DISCOVERED BY: Parker-Foulke, in 1858.

CLASSIFICATION: Ornithischia, Ornithopoda, Hadrosauridae.

REMAINS: discovered in North America.

DIMENSIONS: length: 9 metres.

FOOD: herbivore.

CHARACTERISTICS: *Hadrosaurus* was a herbivorous dinosaur typical of the Cretaceous period. It could stand on either two or four legs and it probably lived in herds. The remains of the *Hadrosaurus* which have been discovered do not enable scientists to reconstruct its appearance accurately because the skull, which is a characteristic feature of all known hadrosaurs, is missing.

The American palaeontologist Joseph Leidy (1823-1891)

Did you know that...

Hadrosaurus was discovered in 1858 by William Parker Foulke, a scientist who had a passion for fossils. The discovery was made in Haddonfield, New Jersey; it included skeletal bones and several teeth but no skull. It was the palaeontologist Joseph Leidy who studied it and named it the following year; Hadrosaurus became a real celebrity because it was the first species of dinosaur described in the United States on the basis of more or less complete remains: an event which made its mark on the world of science and changed our vision of natural history forever.

DINO QUIZ:

Why are *hadrosaurs* called 'duck-billed dinosaurs'?

Because their skull structure and wide, flat mouth were reminiscent of those of today's ducks.

past and present

Near the site in Haddonfield, New Jersey, where the skeleton of the *Hadrosuarus* was discovered, a bronze column has been erected to commemorate the important event.

HAPLOCANTHOSAURUS

NAME *Haplocanthosaurus* means 'lizard with one spine'.

DISCOVERED BY: Hatcher, in 1903.

CLASSIFICATION: Saurischia, Sauropoda, Cetiosauridae.

REMAINS: discovered in North America.

DIMENSIONS: length: 21.5 metres
height: 10.7 metres

FOOD: herbivore.

CHARACTERISTICS: *Haplocanthosaurus* was an animal which spent a large part of its time searching for leaves and shoots and then pulling them off the tops of trees. It had a long neck with 14 vertebrae and a long tail which it used like a whip. Its body was enormous and cumbersome and its head tiny.

Did you know that...

All the Haplocanthosaurus skeletons discovered have been without a head, so scientists have been forced to reconstruct its appearance on the basis of skulls of other similar dinosaurs.

DINO QUIZ:

Why was *Haplocanthosaurus* so called?

The name was inspired by the structure of its vertebrae: each vertebra of the *Haplocanthosaurus* was a single spine, not double and bifurcated like those of most sauropods.

past and present

The skeleton of the great *Haplocanthosaurus*, unfortunately discovered without its head, was found by accident by a lucky young student called Edwin Delfs. It was then entrusted to the palaeontologist John Bell Hatcher who began to study it in 1901 and classified it in 1903.

HARPYMIMUS

NAME: *Harpymimus*, 'mimic of the harpies', owes its name to a monstrous creature in Greek mythology.
The harpies were winged demons with the face of a maiden and the body of a bird.

DISCOVERED BY: Barsbold and Perle, in 1984.

CLASSIFICATION: Saurischia, Theropoda, Harpymimidae.

REMAINS: discovered in Asia.

DIMENSIONS: length: 2 metres
weight: 125 kilograms.

FOOD: probably omnivore.

CHARACTERISTICS: *Harpymimus* was an extremely fast-running biped, with long, thin legs and a slight frame. Its hands were slender with three digits.
It had a beak and about ten small cone-shaped teeth, placed at the front of the lower jaw, which were probably used only to catch and hold its prey. It is not known exactly what *Harpymimus* ate but it is likely that it consumed insects, other small animals and some kinds of plants.

Did you know that...

This dinosaur is the most primitive member of the ornithomimids of Mongolia where it lived about 120 million years ago. Unlike other ornithomimids which had no teeth, Harpymomus had 10 small cylindrical teeth at the front of the lower jaw. This feature makes it a unique and mysterious dinosaur.

NOW, AS THEN ...

There are many omnivorous animals among mammals such as bears, hedgehogs, mice, armadillos, **foxes** and guinea pigs. Among the birds there are the swans, chickens and magpies. Among fish, chub, carp and tench are omnivorous. Among the crustaceans we have prawns, **crabs** and so on. Among insects, the **ants**. In fact, there are omnivorous creatures at all levels of the animal classification, including humans.

DINO QUIZ:

What did *Harpymimus* use its arms for?

According to some scientists it used its front legs to pull the branches of the trees towards it so as to be able to eat them.

HeRReRaSauRuS

NAME: The first fossil remains of *Herrerasaurus* were discovered in 1958 by Victorino Herrera, after whom the dinosaur was named.

DISCOVERED BY: Herrera and then first described by Reig, in 1963.

CLASSIFICATION: Saurischia, Theropoda, Herrerasauridae.

REMAINS: discovered in South America.

DIMENSIONS: length: 4 metres
height: 1.5 metres.

FOOD: carnivore.

CHARACTERISTICS: *Herrerasaurus* was a dinosaur with a slender but powerful build; it had a fairly long neck and long, strong hind legs, while the front limbs had hands with articulated digits used to catch its prey, which it then tore to pieces with its sharp, pointed teeth. *Herrerasaurus* probably preyed on rhyncosaurs which were strange reptiles with a beak, very fat and slow.

Did you know that...

Herrerasaurus was one of the first dinosaurs that existed on Earth; it lived in South America at the end of the Triassic period.
Like all primitive dinosaurs, it was a carnivore and a biped; one of the reasons for the long survival of dinosaurs was their ability to move quickly on two legs.

DINO QUIZ:

How many digits were there on the hands of *Herrerasaurus*?

Like all primitive dinosaurs, *Herrerasaurus* had hands with five digits. Gradually, in the course of evolution the number of digits on dinosaur hands decreased until eventually there were dinosaurs with only one digit.

The skull of *Herrerasaurus*.

past and present

For palaeontologists it is very important to understand how and why dinosaurs disappeared — and it is therefore vital to know the characteristics of the most primitive dinosaurs.

According to many scientists, dinosaurs such as *Herrerasaurus* evolved from tecodont reptiles, similar to crocodiles in appearance but with legs placed directly under the body and teeth strongly anchored into the jaw.

Dinosaurs evolved from tecodont reptiles.

HETERODONTOSAURUS

NAME: *Heterodontosaurus* means 'reptile with different teeth'. This dinosaur had in fact three kinds of teeth in its mouth.

DISCOVERED BY: Crompton and Charig in 1962.

CLASSIFICATION: Ornithischia, Ornithopoda, Heterodontosauridae.

REMAINS: discovered in South-Africa.

DIMENSIONS: length: 1 metre.

FOOD: herbivore.

CHARACTERISTICS: *Heterodontosaurus* must have been a good runner. It was a biped and had a long tail which helped it keep its balance while running and 'sprung' hind legs with articulated feet. The front limbs were sturdy and had five digits with sharp claws. The first digit was particularly lethal because the claw was sickle-shaped. In spite of being a herbivore, *Heterodontosaurus* had four canines protruding from its mouth, two on the upper jaw and two on the lower jaw. These canines must have been either a defence against predators or a sexual signal to females. To tear the leaves off the trees, *Heterodontosaurus* used the incisors at the front of its jaw but for chewing it used the back teeth which were similar to molars.

Did you know that...

Heterodontosaurus was a small herbivorous dinosaur which lived in the Lower Jurassic period in regions corresponding to southern Africa today.
Its main characteristic was that, in spite of being a herbivore, it had four sharp canine teeth which protruded from its mouth.

? DINO QUIZ:

From which predators did *Heterodontosaurus* have to defend itself?

In particular from *Coelophysis*, small, very agile carnivorous dinosaurs which hunted in groups.

NOW, AS THEN ...

Heterodontosaurs had three kinds of teeth, like mammals: canines and incisors at the front and molars at the back for chewing the more fibrous plants.
They may also have had cheeks for accumulating and storing the food.

HOMALOCEPHALE

NAME: *Homalocephale* means 'reptile with flattened head'.

DISCOVERED BY: Maryanska and Osmólska, in 1974.

CLASSIFICATION: Ornithischia, Marginocephalia, Pachycephalosauridae.

REMAINS: discovered in Asia.

DIMENSIONS: length: 2.5 metres
height: 1 metre.

FOOD: herbivore.

CHARACTERISTICS: *Homalocephale* had a thick, flattened cranial roof with irregularly shaped nodules along the back edges of its head and near its mouth.
The teeth were adapted to chewing vegetation, the front legs were short and the tail rigid. *Homalocephale* was not a particularly fast dinosaur; it tended to walk on two legs but to stand and move on four legs when feeding on low vegetation.

Did you know that...

Homalocephale *was a herbivorous dinosaur with a thickened skull. It probably lived in small groups of a few individuals and perhaps used its head, covered in nodules, as a weapon by thrusting it violently into the flank of its opponent. Its strong back and long legs acted as shock-absorbers, also absorbing the impact of its violent head-butts.*

The thickened cranial roof of *Homalocephale*.

past and present

For a long time it was thought that the thickened skulls of pachycephalosaurs were used in fights between males to establish their dominance or as a defence against predators. This idea was first put forward in 1955 by the palaeontologist Colbert. Later, scientists discovered an almost complete *Homalocephale* skeleton and as a result succeeded in producing a very accurate reconstruction of this dinosaur. They agreed that the bones of its skull were particularly full of blood vessels: the skull was therefore not rigid and solid but porous and fragile. It is therefore no longer certain that *Homalocephale* used its head as a weapon.

DINO QUIZ:

Where did the herds of *Homalocephale* dinosaurs live?

It is thought that *Homalocephale* could live in either coastal or mountainous regions.

HYLAEOSAURUS

NAME: *Hylaeosaurus* means 'woodland lizard'.

DISCOVERED BY: Mantell, in 1833.

CLASSIFICATION: Ornithischia, Thyreophora, Nodosauridae.

REMAINS: discovered in Europe.

DIMENSIONS: length: 4 metres.

FOOD: herbivore.

CHARACTERISTICS: *Hylaeosaurus* had a horny beak without teeth and a narrow head with a pointed snout. Its legs were short and sturdy and its tail long and heavy. On its back and sides it had hard, horny, oval-shaped plates implanted in the skin which formed a hard armour covering the upper part of the body and forming a useful protection against predators. Only its belly remained unprotected, so to shield it, *Hylaeosuarus* had to crawl close to the ground.

Did you know that...

Hylaeosaurus *was an armoured, quadruped herbivore dinosaur which lived at the beginning of the Cretaceous period, about 125 million years ago. Its appearance is reminiscent of the famous Ankylosaurus but more primitive. It did not have a horn on top of its head or a club at the end of its tail.*

DINO QUIZ:

Was *Hylaeosaurus* an intelligent dinosaur?

Hylaeosaurus was a member of the family of the nodosaurs, one of the groups of dinosaurs with the lowest IQ.

past and Present

Hylaeosaurus was the third dinosaur to be classified – as long ago as 1833 – by the English palaeontologist Gideon Mantell.

HYPACROSAURUS

NAME: *Hypacrosaurus* means 'near the highest lizard', referring to the high rounded crest on its head.

DISCOVERED BY: Brown, in 1913.

CLASSIFICATION: Ornithischia, Ornithopoda, Hadrosauridae.

REMAINS: originated in North America.

DIMENSIONS: length: 9 metres.

FOOD: herbivore.

CHARACTERISTICS: *Hypacrosaurus* was a large herbivorous dinosaur with a big flattened mouth, similar to a duck's bill and a high, hollow rounded crest on its head. It had hundreds of teeth arranged in many rows which were used for grinding and chewing into a mush the plant matter it fed on. It walked mostly on two legs but could occasionally walk as a quadruped. Its arms were shorter than its legs and its tail was long and heavy. It had nothing to defend itself with but could run extremely fast and so escape from any predator. The vertebrae of its spinal column had rather tall spines; it is probable that these structures controlled a kind of sail which, seen in profile, gave him a 'larger' appearance, thus scaring predators.

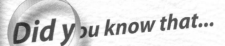

Did you know that...

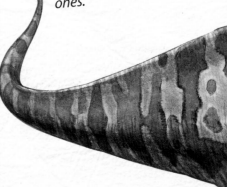

Hypacrosaurus *had a high crest, almost triangular in shape, which resembled a strange, flattened, hollow helmet. Because its nostrils extended into this hollow crest, experts believed that this structure might have been used as a resonance chamber to produce sounds, or as a cooling device, or for decoration, or to amplify olfactory sensations. Possibly the males had larger crests than females and young ones.*

DINO QUIZ:

What did Hypacrosaurus eat?

Probably grains, fruit, conifer shoots and magnolia leaves.

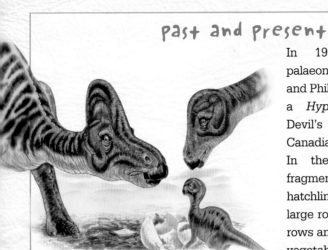

past and present

In 1994, the American palaeontologists Jack Horner and Philip J. Currie discovered a *Hypacrosaurus* nest in Devil's Coulee, within the Canadian province of Alberta. In the **nest** they found fragments of bones of many hatchlings as well as eight large round eggs, arranged in rows and covered in sand and vegetable matter.

HYPSILOPHODON

NAME: The name *Hypsilophodon* means 'high-crested tooth'.

DISCOVERED BY: Huxley, in 1869.

CLASSIFICATION: Ornithischia, Ornithopoda, Hypsilophodontidae.

REMAINS: found in the United States, England and the Iberian peninsula.

DIMENSIONS: length: 2 metres
height: 60 centimetres
weight: 68 kilograms.

FOOD: herbivore.

CHARACTERISTICS: *Hypsilophodon* had the characteristics of a primitive dinosaur despite living in the Mesozoic era. It was a fast-running biped with long, agile rear legs, a rigid tail which helped its balance and large eyes. It had a horny beak and about 30 grinding teeth, arranged in a row. Its hands had five digits and its feet four toes. The back of this dinosaur was protected by a light armour.

Did you know that...

In 1870, the palaeontologist Thomas Huxley described Hypsilophodon as a tree-climbing dinosaur: its small size, long tail and hands with five digits gave it the appearance of a tree-climbing kangaroo, leading scientists to believe that it could climb trees. In 1974 the palaeontologist Peter M. Galton re-examined the remains and proved that neither the hands, feet nor tail of Hypsilophodon could be prehensile. A century after its discovery it was finally realised that Hypsilophodon was in reality a terrestrial dinosaur.

NOW, AS THEN ...

The female *Hypsilophodon* laid eggs and looked after its young. This maternal care is demonstrated by the careful arrangement of the eggs in the **nests**.
Many birds today still behave in the same way.

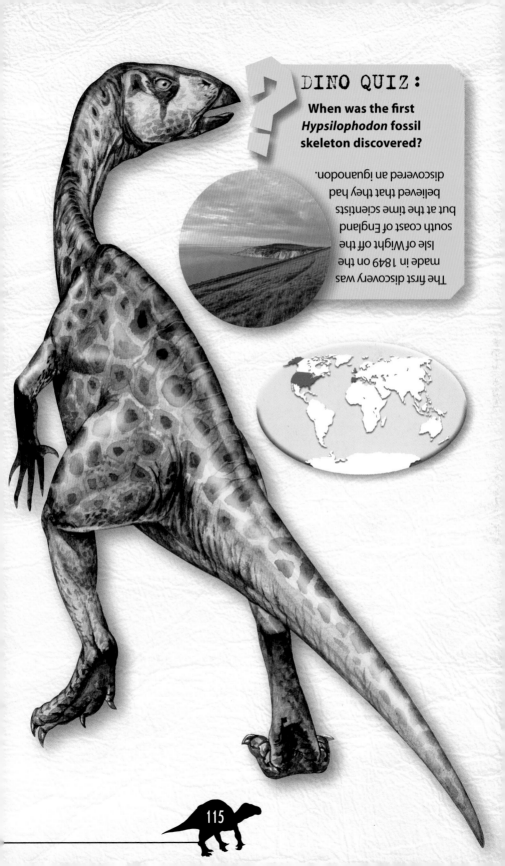

DINO QUIZ:

When was the first *Hypsilophodon* fossil skeleton discovered?

The first discovery was made in 1849 on the Isle of Wight off the south coast of England but at the time scientists believed that they had discovered an iguanodon.

IGUANODON

NAME: *Iguanodon* means 'iguana tooth' and is so called for the presumed similarity between its teeth and those of the iguana of today.

DISCOVERED BY: Mantell, in 1825.

CLASSIFICATION: Ornithischia, Ornithopoda, Iguanodontidae.

REMAINS: discovered in Europe, America, Africa and Asia.

DIMENSIONS: length: 10 metres
height: 5 metres
weight: 5 tonnes.

FOOD: herbivore.

CHARACTERISTICS: *Iguanodon* was a herbivorous dinosaur with a hard beak for cutting vegetation, cheeks for hoarding food and numerous grinding teeth in the rear part of its mouth. It had an elongated skull of remarkable size, two large nasal openings and large eyes. Normally it moved as a quadruped but it could stand up on it rear legs to reach the highest foliage or to run. The powerful limbs ended in a foot with three digits, long and powerful, with nails transformed into hoofs that were useful for galloping. The hands too had hoofs but only on the three central digits; the fifth digit was small and prehensile, while the first had a strong claw, used for defence or for obtaining food. *Iguanadon* defended itself from predators by herding together, running fast and using their lethal thumbs.

Did you know that...

Iguanodon was one of the first dinosaurs to be discovered, it is the best-known and it was the most widely distributed herbivore during the Cretaceous period. It was also the first to be reconstructed; a reproduction was made by the painter Hawkins under the guidance of the palaeontologist Owen and was then exhibited at the Crystal Palace in London but it was not accurate because Iguanodon was shown as a dumpy lizard-like quadruped with a horn on its nose.

DINO QUIZ:

What species of *Iguanodon* are known?

The remains of *Iguanodon* are very common and abundant because this genus was rich in species; the best known are *Iguanodon bernissartensis*, very large and strong and *Iguanodon atherfieldensis*, very small.

past and present

The first fossils of iguanodons were discovered in 1822 in Lewes, England, by Mary Ann Mantell, wife of the doctor, geologist and fossil enthusiast Gideon Mantell, who undertook their study. The first reconstruction of *Iguanodon*, suggested by Mantell, described a strange lizard-like creeping creature with a horn on its nose (this horn would later turn out to be a claw of the hand). Then in 1854 Owen modified the first interpretation by transforming *Iguanodon* into a quadruped lizard which walked on erect legs but still with a horn on its nose. Towards the end of the 19th century, as a result of more complete finds, this animal was pictured as a powerful biped and the horn was at last placed in its rightful position: on the thumb. The most recent reconstructions present *Iguanodon* as a predominantly quadruped animal which ran at high speed with a bipedal gait only when necessary.

INDOSUCHUS

NAME: *Indosuchus* means 'Indian crocodile'.

DISCOVERED BY: von Huene and Matley, in 1933.

CLASSIFICATION: Saurischia, Theropoda, Abelisauridae.

REMAINS: discovered in India.

DIMENSIONS: length: 7 metres
height: 4.5 metres.

FOOD: carnivore.

CHARACTERISTICS: *Indosuchus* was a carnivorous dinosaur of the family of abelisaurids which lived at the end of the Cretaceous period, about 70 million years ago. It had a powerful structure and it moved as a biped. It had numerous serrated teeth and a narrow skull. It is known only from a few pieces of a large skull found in India by the researcher Charles Matley.

Did you know that...

The first remains of Indosuchus were described in about 1930 by the palaeontologist von Huene, who mistook them for fossils of a primitive tyrannosaur. In the 1980s, when remains of several large carnivores came to light in South America, it was possible to establish the true nature of Indosuchus and it was placed in a group of primitive predators: the abelisaurids.

What did the Earth look like when *Indosuchus* lived?

In the Cretaceous period the Earth did not have the same appearance as it does today. India, where *Indosuchus* was discovered, was still joined to Madagascar and South America but was separated from the Eurasian continent to which it is now connected.

Past and Present

Indosuchus was discovered in the Indian region of Madhaya Pradesh. This is the largest state in India: to the north, its territory extends across the Ganges plain; to the south, it rises up in the centre, with hills and plateaux covered by luxuriant **forests**, the habitat of tigers, panthers and Indian bison. Tribal peoples live in the forests in small villages where they follow ancestral customs and traditions.

Jaxartosaurus

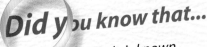

NAME: *Jaxartosaurus* means 'Jaxartes lizard', from the name of the Jaxartes river in Kazakhstan, where it was discovered.

DISCOVERED BY: Riabinin, in 1937.

CLASSIFICATION: Ornithischia, Ornithopoda, Hadrosauridae.

REMAINS: found in Asia.

DIMENSIONS: length: 9 metres
height: 5 metres.

FOOD: herbivore.

CHARACTERISTICS: *Jaxartosaurus* was a dinosaur with a duck's beak of substantial size but palaeontologists know little about it.
Like all the hadrosaurs, it was an optional biped, with strong teeth arranged in rows and a small hollow crest on the top of its head. Some characteristics suggest that *Jaxartosaurus* was a fairly primitive hadrosaur.

Did you know that...

Very little is known about this dinosaur because only a few fragments of its skull have been found. The head would appear to be very similar to that of another dinosaur with a duck's beak and crested head, Corythosaurus.

NOW, AS THEN ...

The articulation of the jaw of *Jaxartosaurus* was similar to that of modern **crocodiles**. It was a structure jointed in such a way that it could function as a shock-absorber when the mouth abruptly snapped shut.

DINO QUIZ:

How many million years ago did *Jaxartosaurus* live?

Fossils of *Jaxartosaurus* date back to 91-84 million years ago, that is, to the Upper Cretaceous period.

KenTROSAURUS

NAME: *Kentrosaurus* means 'lizard with spines'.

DISCOVERED BY: Enning, in 1915.

CLASSIFICATION: Ornithischia, Thyreophora, Stegosauridae.

REMAINS: found in East Africa.

DIMENSIONS: length: 5 metres
weight: 2 tonnes.

FOOD: herbivore.

CHARACTERISTICS: As well as plates on the front part of its back, *Kentrosaurus* had some bony spines on its back, tail and shoulders. The ones on its shoulders pointed outwards and served to protect the animal against attacks from the side. The enormous stomach of *Kentrosaurus* was needed to digest the large quantity of coriaceous (leathery) plants on which it fed. The head, on the other hand, was extremely small, high and narrow; it contained a brain the size of a walnut. The muzzle terminated in a horny beak and in its mouth were some tiny grinding teeth. *Kentrosaurus* moved as a quadruped but the rear legs were substantially longer than the front ones.

Did you know that...

Kentrosaurus, like all stegosaurs, had a very small brain, weighing about 70 grams. However, other small 'additional brains' were placed at various points along the bone marrow and served to increase the speed of nervous impulses. As a result of this system, Kentrosaurus was capable of better controlling the movements of its legs and tail which were, with its spines, its main defensive weapons.

past and present

Numerous fossil skeletons belonging to *Kentrosaurus* have come to light on the hill of Tendaguru in Tanzania, near the remains of several dinosaurs of the genus *Giraffatitan*.

DINO QUIZ:

Have remains of *Kentrosaurus* been found only in the African continent?

No, it appears that a North American species of this dinosaur may also exist but this is still not a proven fact.

LaMBEOSAURUS

NAME: *Lambeosaurus* means 'Lamb's lizard', so named after the Canadian palaeontologist, Lamb.

DISCOVERED BY: Parks, in 1923.

CLASSIFICATION: Ornithischia, Ornithopoda, Lambeosauridae.

REMAINS: found in Central and North America.

DIMENSIONS: length: 15 metres
weight: 6 tonnes.

FOOD: herbivore.

CHARACTERISTICS: *Lambeosaurus* was a hadrosaur which was distinguished by a curious crest on its head. It moved like a quadruped but if necessary it was capable of running very fast on its hind legs. Its speed in flight together with its well-developed sight and hearing were its main defences against predators. *Lambeosaurus* had about a hundred small teeth to grind tough vegetable matter such as pine needles, grains and woody shoots. The worn-out teeth were soon replaced by new ones. Its muzzle was narrow and ended in a wide, blunt beak.

Did you know that...

With a length of 15 metres, Lambeosaurus was the largest known duck-billed dinosaur. Its head was two metres long and crowned by a curious axe-shaped crest, the weight of which must certainly have exceeded that of the skull which supported it.

The zebra is perfectly adapted to running. During the course of its evolution the zebra's legs changed drastically, leading to the regression and then the complete disappearance of some digits.

The only remaining functional digit, the third one, is very sturdy and well developed, ending with a strong claw: the hoof.

NOW, AS THEN ...

The legs of *Lambeosaurus* terminated with claws transformed into hoofs as in today's **ungulate mammals** of the savannah, animals which live in very wide open spaces and are well adapted to running.

DINO QUIZ:

What was the use of the large, strange crest of *Lambeosaurus*?

Scientists do not agree on the function of the crest of the *Lambeosaurus* (or that of any hadrosaur). Some believe that it helped the hadrosaur to breathe while underwater; others think that the crest was used to produce a characteristic sound, similar to that of a medieval horn; others believe that this crest increased the sense of smell; while yet others are of the opinion that it served to attract a mate during courtship.

Leaellynasaurus

NAME: *Leaellynasaurus* means 'Leaellyn's lizard', named after Leaellyn Rich, the 11-year old daughter of the couple who discovered and studied it, Tom and Patricia Rich.

DISCOVERED BY: T. Rich and P. Rich, in 1989.

CLASSIFICATION: Ornithischia, Ornithopoda, Hypsilophodontidae.

REMAINS: discovered in south-eastern Australia.

DIMENSIONS: length: 1 metre
height: 50 centimetres.

FOOD: herbivore.

CHARACTERISTICS: *Leaellynasaura* was a herbivorous hypsilophodontid which moved nimbly on its long hind legs and used its great speed to escape from predators.

Did you know that...

Remains of this dinosaur were discovered in south-eastern Australia. It was a partial skeleton of a young dinosaur with an almost complete skull and many small scattered bones, about 75 centimetres long and 30 centimetres high. The adults probably reached a length of 1 metre.

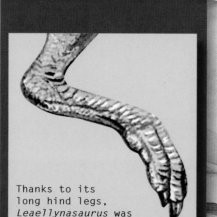

Thanks to its long hind legs, *Leaellynasaurus* was able to run very fast.

DINO QUIZ:

What was the environment in Australia like when *Leaellynasaurus* lived there?

Leaellynasaurus probably lived in cold conifer forests.

past and Present

Today Australia with its hot climate is separated from the cold continent of Antarctica by an ocean but in the Cretaceous period, about 100 million years ago, these two continents were joined. At the time there was no snow or ice on Earth but the nights could be long and dinosaurs which lived near the South Pole, such as *Leaellynasaurus*, must have adapted to cold temperatures, mud and the long winter nights. The metabolism of these dinosaurs must therefore have been different from that of the lizard today and their eyes had to be big to see clearly during the long winter periods when the night could last several months.

LeptoceratopS

NAME: *Leptoceratops* means 'lean-horned face'.

DISCOVERED BY: Brown, in 1914.

CLASSIFICATION: Ornithischia, Marginocephalia, Ceratopsidae.

REMAINS: discovered in North America.

DIMENSIONS: length: 2 metres
height: 75 centimetres
weight: 68 kilograms.

FOOD: herbivore.

CHARACTERISTICS: *Leptoceratops* was a small dinosaur which normally walked as a quadruped but was able to walk as a biped.
It was fairly nimble as a result of its long legs. Unlike its relatives, the other Ceratopsians, its large skull had no horn apart from a single one on the back of its neck facing backwards. There was a kind of bony ruff on the back of its head. It had small prehensile hands to grab hold of the low branches of bushes and a sharp beak (similar to that of a parrot) with which to cut them.

Did you know that...

Leptoceratops *was a primitive ceratopsian dinosaur in spite of the fact that it lived during the Late Cretaceous period. Its famous giant relatives, such as* Triceratops *and* Torosaurus, *were its contemporaries.*

The paws of the panda of today have evolved so as to be prehensile (grasping) and so can grab the bamboo branches upon which it feeds.

DINO QUIZ:

How many species of *Leptoceratops* are there?

There are two species:
Leptoceratops gracilis and
Leptoceratops cerorhynchus.

The skull of
Leptoceratops.

past and present

The first remains of *Leptoceratops* were found in Alberta in 1910 but they were incomplete. In 1947 better-preserved remains were found which included a complete skull. In 1978 another skeleton was discovered in Wyoming.

LesoTHosauRus

NAME: *Lesothosaurus* means 'lizard from Lesotho', after the place where it was discovered.

DISCOVERED BY: Galton, in 1978.

CLASSIFICATION: Ornithischia, Ornithopoda, Fabrosauridae.

REMAINS: discovered in South Africa.

DIMENSIONS: length: 1 metre
weight: 10 kilograms.

FOOD: herbivore.

CHARACTERISTICS: *Lesothosaurus* was a small, light dinosaur, an agile, very fast-running biped with long, powerful legs. It had four toes on its feet and five digits on its hands. Its arms were short, its neck and tail were long and it had a small head with large eyes. Its teeth were leaf-shaped to grind the plant matter upon which it fed.

Did you know that...

Lesothosaurus *lived during the period straddling the end of the Triassic and the beginning of the Jurassic, about 200 million years ago. It was one of the most primitive known ornithischian dinosaurs. Its skeleton includes several primitive features such as hands with five digits and the absence of cheeks (which later animals found useful for holding as much food as possible).*

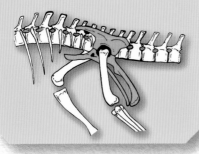
past and present

Palaeontologists are almost always dealing with a very small number of fragments of animals which lived millions and millions of years ago, so they can never be certain of their theories. For example, in the 1960s a fossil fragment of a jaw was discovered in Lesotho which was attributed to the genus *Fabrosaurus*. Some ten years later *Lesothosaurus* was discovered. Scientists discovered a great resemblance to the *Fabrosaurus* and believed it was the same animal. Unfortunately there were so few fragments to work with that it was impossible to say with certainty whether or not they were two different animals.

LIAONINGOSAURUS

latest discovery

NAME: *Liaoningosaurus* means 'lizard of Liaoning', after the Chinese province where it was found.

DISCOVERED BY: Xu, Wang and You in 2001.

CLASSIFICATION: Ornithischia, Thyreophora.

REMAINS: discovered in Asia.

DIMENSIONS: length: 34 centimetres.

FOOD: herbivore.

CHARACTERISTICS: *Liaoningosaurus* had bony spikes or nodules all over its body which formed a rigid protective armour. The feature which distinguishes it most from the other armoured dinosaurs is the presence of hexagonal or rhombic osteoderms (bony deposits) even on its belly.

Did you know that...

Liaoningosaurus was an unusual armoured dinosaur. A complete, well-preserved fossil skeleton has been found belonging to a young dinosaur only 34 centimetres long — the smallest ankylosaur in the world, so far as we know!

132

DINO QUIZ:

Where is the only *Liaoningosaurus* fossil skeleton preserved?

The only *Liaoningosaurus* skeleton is kept at the Institute of Vertebrate Palaeontology and Palaeoanthropology in Beijing, the capital of the People's Republic of China.

The Sacred Way in the city of Beijing.

Past and Present

Palaeontologists have recently discovered fossil remains of the greatest scientific importance in the Chinese province of Liaoning. In particular the discovery of feathered dinosaurs which once lived in the Early Cretaceous has completely revolutionised theories of the evolution of life on our planet and thrown light on one of the greatest mysteries: the origin of the birds.

LILIENSTERNUS

NAME: *Liliensternus* takes its name from the German scientist H. Rühle von Lilienstern.

DISCOVERED BY: Welles, in 1984.

CLASSIFICATION: Saurischia, Theropoda, Coelophysoidea.

REMAINS: discovered in Europe.

DIMENSIONS: length: 5 metres
height: 2 metres.

FOOD: carnivore.

CHARACTERISTICS: *Liliensternus* was a biped predator with a nimble, light skeleton, very similar to that of the *Coelophysis*. It had long legs and two bony crests on its head, like those on the head of the *Dilophosaurus*.

Did you know that...

Liliensternus was almost certainly the largest carnivorous dinosaur of its time. It was very primitive but with a length of 5 metres it was considerably larger than Coelophysis and Syntarsus which were its contemporaries. It ate small lizards and amphibians but could also join in groups to hunt young prosauropods such as Plateosaurus.

DINO QUIZ:

Where were the remains of *Liliensternus* first discovered?

The remains of *Liliensternus* were first discovered in Germany.

Liliensternus adopted a hunting technique similar to that used by the big cats today.

NOW, AS THEN ...

Many carnivores today, for instance the **big cats**, hunt on their own or in groups. Hunting in groups makes it possible for predators to catch more difficult prey which would be impossible or dangerous for a single individual to pursue.

MAIASAURA

NAME: *Maiasaura* means 'good mother lizard'; it is thought that it looked after its young lovingly.

DISCOVERED BY: Horner and Makela, in 1979.

CLASSIFICATION: Ornithischia, Ornithopoda, Hadrosauridae.

REMAINS: discovered in North America.

DIMENSIONS: length: 9 metres
height: 2.5 metres
weight: 4 tonnes.

FOOD: herbivore.

CHARACTERISTICS: *Maiasaura* had a wide, flattened snout, similar to the beak of a duck, and a small spiky crest between the eyes; its jaws had many rows of serrated teeth which were perfect for mincing and grinding the fibrous plant matter it ate.
It migrated long distances in search of plants to eat and safe places in which to form colonies where nests would be built.
It was capable of looking after its young lovingly. It lived in herds of thousands of animals to discourage predators; if attacked it stood on its powerful hind legs and could escape at great speed.

Did you know that...

In Montana, North America, a site was discovered with over 40 nests and the fossil remains of about 10,000 Maiasaura. Adult Maiasaura remains have been discovered next to the skeletons of their young, and fossilized eggs and nests.
This seems to suggest that Maiasaura ministered to the needs of its young.
The round nest was dug into the ground. It had a diameter of about 2 metres and could contain up to 25 eggs, each the size of a grapefruit. The young were about 30 centimetres long at birth and remained near the nests, probably because they were fed, protected and looked after by the parents: the distance between the nests was sufficient to enable Maiasaura adults to move around and pass by them.

DINO QUIZ:

How much did a large herbivore dinosaur such as *Maiasaura* eat in one day?

An adult could consume about 90 kilograms of leaves, shoots, berries and grains every day.

past and present

The bone of a *Maiasaura* and part of the shell of one its eggs were taken into space by the astronaut Loren Acton in 1985 on the Spacelab 2 mission which lasted eight days. *Maiasaura* is certainly the first dinosaur to have travelled into space.

MAMENCHISAURUS

NAME: *Mamenchisaurus* means 'lizard of Mamenchi', the name of the Chinese locality where it was discovered.

DISCOVERED BY: Young, in 1954.

CLASSIFICATION: Saurischia, Sauropoda, Euhelopodidae.

REMAINS: discovered in Asia.

DIMENSIONS: length: 26 metres
height: 5 metres
weight: 40 tonnes.

FOOD: herbivore.

CHARACTERISTICS: *Mamenchisaurus* was a herbivorous dinosaur with a very long neck and a tiny head. It moved on four thick, pillar-like legs and was longer than a tennis court but with a rather thin build. Its skeleton was lighter than might be expected because its spine was hollow. Its very long tail acted as a balance and also as an effective weapon with its whip-like end. The first digit of its front legs had a powerful, lethal claw. The numerous fossil footmarks show that *Mamenchisaurus* lived in large family groups with many individuals.

Did you know that...

Mamenchisaurus had by far the longest neck ever seen in an animal! The 19 cervical neck vertebrae had ribs which anchored them to each other and to the tendons, thus making it easier to flex the neck. The powerful muscles of its back enabled Mamenchisaurus to raise its neck to an almost vertical position.

DINO QUIZ:

How long was the neck of *Mamenchisaurus*?

The neck of *Mamenchisaurus* was over 15 metres long, making this the longest neck of any animal that has ever lived on Earth.

138

NOW, AS THEN ...

Like **elephants** today, *Mamenchisuarus* lived in family groups led by a female. When the herd migrated, the young travelled in the middle of the group, protected by their mothers on the outside. The males were so large that they feared no danger and could therefore live on their own.

MassosPondylus

NAME: *Massospondylus* means 'voluminous vertebra'.

DISCOVERED BY: Owen, in 1854.

CLASSIFICATION: Saurischia, Prosauropoda, Massospondylidae.

REMAINS: discovered in Africa and North America.

DIMENSIONS: length: 5 metres
height: 1.5 metres.

FOOD: herbivore.

CHARACTERISTICS: *Massospondylus* was a primitive herbivore dinosaur with a long neck and a long tail. It had a small head, pin-like teeth and hands with five digits with a large articulated thumb. It may have used its front legs to catch things as well as for walking. Its hind legs were slightly longer than the front ones. It is thought that *Massospondylus* was a quadruped, capable of running quite fast although it could also move on just its hind legs for short periods.

The English palaeontologist Richard Owen (1804-1892).

Did you know that...

At the end of the Triassic and the beginning of the Jurassic period, about 200 million years ago, Massospondylus was one of the most widespread herbivore dinosaurs. Many Massospondylus fossil skeletons have been found so much is known about it. It was also the first dinosaur to be discovered in Africa and one of the first to be studied and described by the English palaeontologist Richard Owen, in 1854.

In South Africa during the 1970s, Massospondylus eggs were discovered which still contained embryos; they are the oldest dinosaur embryos to be found in the world.

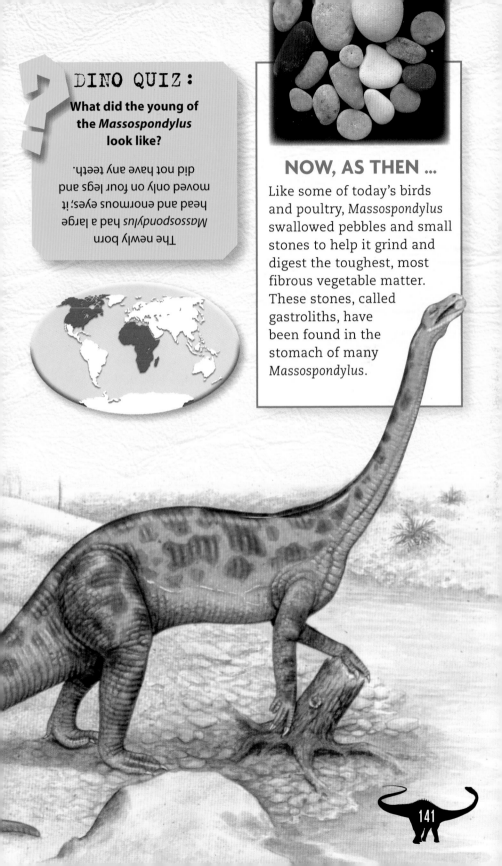

DINO QUIZ:

What did the young of the *Massospondylus* look like?

The newly born *Massospondylus* had a large head and enormous eyes; it moved only on four legs and did not have any teeth.

NOW, AS THEN ...

Like some of today's birds and poultry, *Massospondylus* swallowed pebbles and small stones to help it grind and digest the toughest, most fibrous vegetable matter. These stones, called gastroliths, have been found in the stomach of many *Massospondylus*.

141

MEGALOSAURUS

NAME: *Megalosaurus* means 'giant lizard'.

DISCOVERED BY: Buckland, in 1824.

CLASSIFICATION: Saurischia, Theropoda, Megalosauridae.

REMAINS: discovered in Europe.

DIMENSIONS: length: 9 metres
height: 3 metres
weight: 1 tonne.

FOOD: carnivore.

CHARACTERISTICS: *Megalosaurus* was a biped, had a short, muscular neck and a large head with sharp, serrated teeth. Its tail was rather thick and the fore limbs had three digits with sharp claws.

Did you know that...

Megalosaurus *was one of the most dangerous predators that lived during the Jurassic period in Europe and one of the most primitive* Tetanurae.

It is known only through the fossil remains of a lower jawbone with teeth, vertebrae, fragments of pelvis, scapula and hind leg bones.

A study of the jaw of a *Megalosaurus* by William Buckland.

Past and Present

Megalosaurus was the first dinosaur to be discovered, in England in 1819, and it was studied by the scientist William Buckland in 1824. Initially it was described as a giant crocodile.

DINO QUIZ:

What were the characteristics of the carnivore dinosaurs known as 'Tetanurae'?

Tetanurae dinosaurs were theropods with three digits on their fore limbs and a rigid tail.

Tetanurae dinosaurs had a long, rigid tail.

MICROCERATOPS

NAME: *Microceratops* means 'small horned face'.

DISCOVERED BY: Bohlin, in 1953.

CLASSIFICATION: Ornithischia, Ceratopsia, Protoceratopsidae.

REMAINS: discovered in Asia.

DIMENSIONS: length: 80 centimetres
height: 60 centimetres
weight: 5 kilograms.

FOOD: Herbivore.

CHARACTERISTICS: *Microceratops* was very small, only a few dozen centimetres long; it was a biped with thin limbs, two short horns and a beak like that of a parrot.

Did you know that...

Microceratops was very similar to another of the small Ceratopsidae, Protoceratops, but even smaller. It lived at the end of the Cretaceous period, between 80 and 65 million years ago, in the part of the world which is now China.

DINO QUIZ:

What did Microceratops eat?

Microceratops mainly ate those plants which were commonest at the time: **cycads** and conifers.

NOW, AS THEN ...

Microceratops is a relative of the most famous of the Ceratopsidae, the giant *Triceratops* and *Styracosaurus*, but it was only the size of a rabbit.

145

MINMI

NAME: It was named *Minmi* after the locality of 'Minmi Crossing' in Australia, where it was discovered.

DISCOVERED BY: Molnar, in 1980.

CLASSIFICATION: Ornithischia, Thyreophora, Nodosauridae.

REMAINS: discovered in Oceania.

DIMENSIONS: length: 3 metres
height: 1 metre.

FOOD: herbivore.

CHARACTERISTICS: *Minmi* walked on four rather dumpy legs; it had a long tail, short neck and a wide skull with a very small brain. The whole of its body, including its belly, was covered by a series of osseous (bony) plates as body armour. Its back and sides were covered by small protuberances; the head too was protected by a thick osseous plate. Unlike the other nodosaurs, *Minmi* had a series of horizontal bony plates that ran along the sides of the vertebrae.

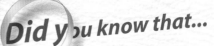

Did you know that...

Minmi *was a small dinosaur with a body covered by bony plates. It was an extremely small dinosaur compared to the other dinosaurs in the same family.*

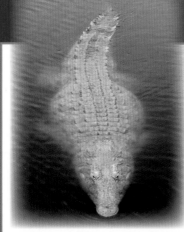

NOW, AS THEN ...

The lateral structure of *Minmi's* vertebrae was probably similar to the lateral tendons of crocodiles; these help keep their backs stiff. Young crocodiles (and perhaps once young *Minmi* too) gallop along surprisingly quickly but adult *Minmi* were probably slow and ponderous.

DINO QUIZ:

Where and when were the first fossil remains of *Minmi* discovered?

The first *Minmi* fossil remains were discovered in 1964 by Alan Bartholomai near Roma, in Queensland, Australia.

The fossilised skeleton of *Minmi*.

147

MONONYCHUS

NAME: *Mononychus* was named 'single claw' because its fore limbs ended in a single sturdy claw.

DISCOVERED BY: Perle, Norell, Chiappe and Clark, in 1993.

CLASSIFICATION: Saurischia, Theropoda, Dromaeosauridae.

REMAINS: discovered in Asia.

DIMENSIONS: length: 1 metre.

FOOD: carnivore.

CHARACTERISTICS: *Mononychus* was a dinosaur the size of a turkey which walked like a biped. It had small sharp teeth, a long neck, a long tail and agile, slender legs perfectly adapted for running. Because of its small size and slender build it is thought that it probably hunted in groups. It did not have wings but many of its features were similar to those of birds: for instance, the bones of its wrist were fused together and its chest housed a 'carinate' breasbone – a keel or ridge to which flight muscles are attached in birds.

Did you know that...

The discovery of *Mononychus* led to a debate among scientists which was never resolved: the important question of whether birds were descended from dinosaurs. The similarities between *Mononychus* and a bird led to the conclusion that birds must belong to the family tree of dinosaurs. Some scientists go so far as to claim that *Mononychus* should be classed among birds and not dinosaurs.

DINO QUIZ:

What is the sternum or breastbone and what is it for?

The sternum is an elongated, flattened bone which connects the rib bones to the rib cage and so closes the thorax. In birds, as in *Mononychus*, the sternum is ridged to provide a better surface for the attachment of powerful flying muscles.

NOW, AS THEN ...

Palaeontologists did not discover a whole *Mononychus* at one site. Various fragments were discovered at different times, in 1923, 1987 and 1992, and our understanding of its anatomy was gathered piece by piece. Palaeontologist Norell finally revealed the results of his research in the **Gobi Desert**, carried out in collaboration with the Academy of Sciences of Mongolia; he presented *Mononychus* to the world in 1993.

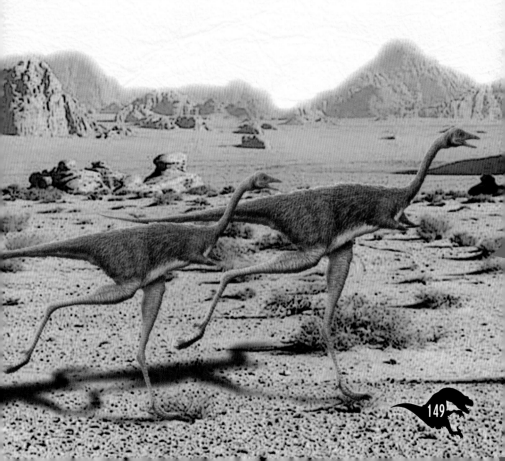

149

MUSSAURUS

NAME: The name means 'rat lizard' because of its small size.

DISCOVERED BY: Bonaparte and Vince, in 1979.

CLASSIFICATION: Saurischia, Prosauropoda, Plateosauridae.

REMAINS: discovered in South America.

DIMENSIONS: length: 37 centimetres.

FOOD: herbivore.

CHARACTERISTICS: *Mussaurus* was a small prosauropod, a primitive herbivore dinosaur. The fossils so far discovered are the skeletons of young specimens. *Mussaurus* had a long neck, a long tail, a small head with big eyes, an elongated snout, large hands with five digits, a powerful claw on the thumb and smaller claws on the other digits. The hind legs were longer than the front ones.

Did you know that...

No fossil remains of adult Mussaurus have been found but only those of very young individuals. They are the smallest dinosaur skeletons ever found and are so tiny that they can fit in a person's hand.

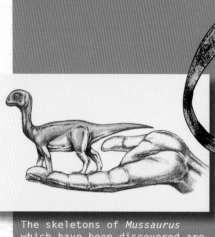

The skeletons of *Mussaurus* which have been discovered are smaller than a man's hand.

NOW, AS THEN ...

Researchers have also discovered fossilised *Mussaurus* eggs: they are only 2.5 centimetres long and more or less the same size as a **quail's eggs**.

DINO QUIZ:

How big would *Mussaurus* have grown as an adult?

As an adult *Mussaurus* might have reached a length of 3 metres and weighed up to 120 kilograms.

151

MUTTABURRASAURUS

NAME: *Muttaburrasaurus* means 'lizard of Muttaburra', named after the site in central Queensland in Australia where the remains were discovered.

DISCOVERED BY: Langdon in 1963 and named by Bartholomai and Molnar, in 1981.

CLASSIFICATION: Ornithischia, Ornithopoda, Rhabdodontidae.

REMAINS: found in Oceania.

DIMENSIONS: length: 7 metres
weight: 3 tonnes.

FOOD: mainly herbivore.

CHARACTERISTICS: *Muttaburrasaurus* was a herbivorous dinosaur, similar to the more famous *Iguanodon*. It had a bulge between the eyes and the mouth, a beak and sharp, pointed teeth like scissors. Its claws had developed into hoofs and it could probably walk on either two or four legs.

Did you know that...

The osseous (bony) protuberance on its nose could be an enlargement of the basal cavity to increase the sense of smell, or it may be associated with the ability to emit sounds to communicate more easily with other members of the group.

DINO QUIZ:

Where are the remains of *Muttaburrasaurus* exhibited?

Reconstructed *Muttaburrasaurus* skeletons are exhibited at the Queensland Museum in Brisbane, the Fukui Prefectural Dinosaur Museum in Katsuyama, Japan, and at the Flinders Discovery Centre at Hughenden in Queensland.

Past and Present

The very first remains of a *Muttaburrasaurus* to be discovered were found in 1963 near Rosebury Downs station on the Thompson River near the city of Muttaburra in Queensland, Australia. They were discovered by a certain Mr. Langdon. The fossils had been trampled on by cattle and some local inhabitants had picked up some pieces and taken them to their homes. When the importance of this discovery was realised, the people were asked to return the fossils. Fortunately many of the bones of the *Muttaburrasaurus* skeleton were then recovered.

153

nanoTYRannus

NAME: *Nanotyrannus* means 'tiny tyrant'.

DISCOVERED BY: Bakker, Williams and Currie, in 1988.

CLASSIFICATION: Saurischia, Theropoda, Tyrannosauridae.

REMAINS: discovered in North America.

DIMENSIONS: length: 6.5 metres
weight: 1 tonne.

FOOD: carnivore.

CHARACTERISTICS: *Nanotyrannus* was a bipedal predator which lived at the end of the Cretaceous period about 68 to 65 million years ago. It had a large head, powerful jaws with sharp teeth, a short, massive neck and long limbs. Only three of the digits on its feet touched the ground when walking. Its arms were short with hands with two digits and it had a thin tail. Its eyes had developed to provide binocular vision and its three-dimensional perception was excellent.

Did you know that...

The only known Nanotyrannus skull was scanned with computerised tomography by the American palaeontologist Robert Bakker. He thought that Nanotyrannus was an adult individual of a genus of dinosaur which was very reminiscent of a Tyrannosaurus but in miniature.

A tooth of *Nanotyrannus*.

DINO QUIZ:

What kind of hunting technique did *Nanotyrannus* use?

Nanotyrannus probably caught its prey directly with its powerful jaws, plunging its sharp, curved teeth into the body of its victim. Perhaps the two very small front limbs, which had powerful claws, could be used to hold its prey so that it could devour it more easily.

Past and Present

The *Nanotyrannus* genus was established in 1988 on the basis of a fossilised skull which had previously been described by the palaeontologist Gilmore as belonging to the genus *Albertosaurus*. It resembles a miniature version of *Tyrannosaurus* but many other palaeontologists, such as Thomas Carr, maintain that the skeleton parts discovered are not completely developed, therefore holding that *Nanotyrannus* is merely a young *Tyrannosaurus*.

155

neimongosaurus

NAME: *Neimongosaurus* means 'lizard of inner Mongolia', after the region where the remains were discovered.

DISCOVERED BY: Zhang, Xu, Sereno, Kuang and Tan, in 2001.

CLASSIFICATION: Saurischia, Theropoda, Therizinosauridae.

REMAINS: discovered in Asia.

DIMENSIONS: length: 4 metres.

FOOD: probably herbivore.

CHARACTERISTICS: *Neimongosaurus* was a strange dinosaur of the Therizinosauridae family, discovered recently. It had an extremely elongated, slender neck, a small skull, minuscule, feeble teeth and a short sturdy tail. It had distinctive and unusual features at the end of its front limbs – very long, lethal claws, the function of which is still uncertain.

Did you know that...

Neimongosaurus was a therizinosaur, a strange group of dinosaurs, also known as segnosaurs, which lived in the Cretaceous period and have been only recently discovered. Therizinosaurs are distinguished by the fact that they display a mixture of features from other groups of dinosaurs, ranging from the primitive prosauropods, to the herbivorous ornithischian dinosaurs and the small and evolved oviraptorids.

The *Neimongosaurus* had vicious long claws on its 'hands'.

past and present

Everything that is known about *Neimongosaurus* is based on two partial fossilised skeletons.

DINO QUIZ:

What did *Neimongosaurus* eat?

Not much is known about the diet of *Neimongosaurus*. Most palaeontologists believe that, in view of the type of teeth, it was probably herbivorous. But other scientists think that it fed on termites and used its very long claws to destroy termites' nests; yet others believe they may have used their enormous claws to spear fish.

neuQuensaurus

NAME: *Neuquensaurus* was called 'Neuquén lizard' after the place where it was discovered.

DISCOVERED BY: J. E. Powell, in 1992.

CLASSIFICATION: Saurischia, Sauropoda, Saltasauridae.

REMAINS: discovered in South America.

DIMENSIONS: length: 15 metres
height: 5 metres.

FOOD: herbivore.

CHARACTERISTICS: *Neuquensaurus* was a large dinosaur of the family of the Saltasauridae. It ate plants, walked as a quadruped, had a long neck and a long tail and was covered with osseous bony plates and nodules which formed a sort of armour on its skin.

Did you know that...

Neuquensaurus *was a dinosaur related to the more famous* Saltasaurus *but it lived a few million years earlier.*

Past and Present

Neuquensaurus was described in 1992 by palaeontologist Jaime Powell, based on the fossilised remains which a century earlier Lydekker had wrongly classified in the genus *Titanosaurus*.

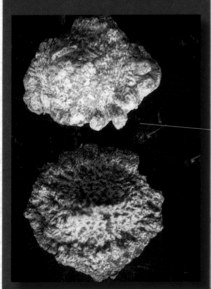

The skin of *Neuquensaurus* was very rigid and hard because of its numerous osseous nodules.

nIGERSaURUS

latest · discovery

NAME: *Nigersaurus* means 'lizard of the Niger'.

DISCOVERED BY: Sereno, Beck, Dutheil, Larsson, Lyon, Moussa, Sadleir, Sidor, Varricchio, G. P. Wilson and J. A. Wilson, in 1999.

CLASSIFICATION: Saurischia, Sauropoda, Rebbachisauridae.

REMAINS: discovered in Africa.

DIMENSIONS: length: 15 metres
height: 3 metres.

FOOD: herbivore.

CHARACTERISTICS: Although *Nigersaurus* belongs to a fairly common species, very little was known about it until recently because of the disjointed state in which the skeletons were found. *Nigersaurus* was a rather primitive sauropod, quadrepedal, with a square snout and long neck. Its weight was less than that of most known sauropods and this, together with its fragile structure, probably made it an easy prey for the large carnivores of the time.

Did you know that...

Nigersaurus *was one of the rare descendants of the Jurassic sauropods (the subgroup to which, for instance, Diplodocus belonged) which lived in the Cretaceous period, about 110 million years ago when most sauropods were already extinct.*

Barren scene in the Niger Desert.

160

past and present

Nigersaurus is one of the commonest dinosaurs found in the rich location for fossilised vertebrate remains discovered by Philippe Taquet in 1976 and known as the Elrahaz Formation in the Republic of Niger. Research scientists **Paul Sereno** and Jeffrey Wilson have described a *Nigersaurus* skull which had 600 very tiny teeth.

NODOSAURUS

NAME: *Nodosaurus* means 'lizard with nodules'. It was given this name because its body was completely covered by osseous (bony) plates and nodules.

DISCOVERED BY: O. C. Marsh, in 1889.

CLASSIFICATION: Ornithischia, Thyreophora, Nodosauridae.

REMAINS: discovered in North America.

DIMENSIONS: length: 6 metres.

FOOD: herbivore.

CHARACTERISTICS: *Nodosaurus* was an armoured dinosaur, stocky, with a massive skull. It was a quadruped with four short, sturdy legs. It was ungainly and slow-moving but is nevertheless considered to have reached a high level of development: to defend itself it crouched on the ground, thus exposing only the simple but effective resistance of its tough armour.

Did you know that...

Nodosaurus *has given its name to the group of dinosaurs of the Nodosauridae family which, unlike the Ankylosauridae which were also armoured, did not have a club at the end of the tail but usually had spikes along the sides.*

DINO QUIZ:

**When was
Nodosaurus discovered?**

Nodosaurus was one of the first
armoured dinosaurs to be discovered,
in 1889, by the palaeontologist
Othniel Charles Marsh.

past and present

Only the remains of three
incomplete *Nodosaurus* skeletons
have been discovered, all of them
without heads and very difficult
to interpret. The few fossils
which have been discovered
are not sufficient to give precise
information on this animal and it is
therefore difficult to reconstruct its
appearance and behaviour.

ORNITHOMIMUS

NAME: *Ornithomimus* means 'bird mimic'.

DISCOVERED BY: O. C. Marsh, in 1890.

CLASSIFICATION: Saurischia, Theropoda, Ornithomimidae.

REMAINS: discovered in North America and Asia.

DIMENSIONS: length: 4 metres
height: 2 metres.

FOOD: omnivore.

CHARACTERISTICS: *Ornithomimus* was an ostrich-dinosaur with a corneous (horny) beak without teeth, a small head, large eyes with a sharp vision and a relatively large brain.
Many bones in the skeleton were hollow and this gave it extreme lightness. The thin, flexible neck and the tail made up half the total length of the body. It had long, thin, flexible legs, ideal for running fast. The forelimbs were short and ended in hands with three articulated digits which were capable of grabbing. The feet also consisted of three long claws, flat and narrow to ensure a good hold on the ground when running. The long and rather inflexible tail acted as a counterweight and as a stabiliser when the animal wanted to turn round fast.

Did you know that...

Ornithomimus *was a very fast and nimble dinosaur; its long, muscular legs enabled it to run as fast as an ostrich of today. This running speed was the only weapon it had to defend itself against predators.* Ornithomimus *was omnivorous; it ate both plants and animals, including insects, small lizards and mammals, eggs and fruit.*

Othniel Charles Marsh (1831-1899), the American palaeontologist who discovered and studied numerous dinosaur fossils.

Past and Present

The first *Ornithomimus* was discovered near to Denver, Colorado, in 1899 and was studied by the palaeontologist Othniel Charles Marsh two years after it was discovered.

OURANOSAURUS

NAME: *Ouranosaurus* means 'Courageous lizard'. Ourano, in the Tuareg language means 'courageous' but it is also the common name of the sand lizard.

DISCOVERED BY: Taquet, in 1976.

CLASSIFICATION: Ornithischia, Ornithopoda, Iguanodontidae.

REMAINS: discovered in North Africa.

DIMENSIONS: length: 7 metres
weight: 4 tonnes.

FOOD: herbivore.

CHARACTERISTICS: *Ouranosaurus* had a long, distinctive sail on its back, running from neck to tail and supported by long vertical spikes which were extensions of the vertebrae. The skull was a little longer than that of the other iguanodontids. It had a small crest on its snout, a flattened beak, wide and without teeth, although it had numerous teeth at the back of its mouth to chew even the toughest plants. Its neck was short and flexible. Each hand had five stumpy fingers, the second and third digits being broad and hoof-like. *Ouranosaurus* was a grazer and it is likely that it was a quadruped. Its thumbs had conical claws which served as its only defence.

Did you know that...

Ouranosaurus was discovered in 1973 during an expedition in the Niger desert, known as the Ligabue expedition because it was directed by the Italian archaeologist Giancarlo Ligabue.
The remains discovered during this expedition are exhibited at the Museum of Natural History in Venice. The distinctive feature of Ouranosaurus was the presence of tall neural (nerve) spines which emerged vertically from the vertebrae. The central spine could reach the considerable height of 70 centimetres.

NOW, AS THEN ...

Like many herbivorous animals today, for instance **antelopes** or gnus, *Ouranosaurus* lived in a group with other dinosaurs of the same species.

166

DINO QUIZ:

What was the role of the dorsal sail of *Ouranosaurus*?

Ouranosaurus probably used its sail to regulate its own body temperature. The sail was used to cool the body down, helping to reduce body temperature more quickly during the day; conversely, in the morning the sail made it possible to absorb the rays of the sun more quickly. The sail may also have been used as a feature to attract females or to frighten a predator by making the creature appear larger than it really was.

167

OVIRAPTOR

NAME: *Oviraptor* means 'robber of eggs' This name was chosen because the first fossil, discovered in Mongolia in 1923, was found next to a nest full of eggs. As a result it was erroneously thought that Oviraptor was killed while trying to steal them.

DISCOVERED BY: Osborn, in 1924.

CLASSIFICATION: Saurischia, Theropoda, Oviraptoridae.

REMAINS: discovered in Asia.

DIMENSIONS: length: 2 metres
height: 1.5 metres
weight: 30 kilograms.

FOOD: omnivore.

CHARACTERISTICS: *Oviraptor* was a fast and clever biped dinosaur. It had a short skull with very curbed jaws and large eyes. The skulls discovered are not all the same: some have an osseous (bony) protuberance above the nostrils while others have a large crest instead. The hands ended in three digits with curved claws, very sharp and about eight centimetres long. It used these three digits to grab its prey. The rear legs were long and supported by powerful muscles. The feet had three powerful, articulated digits.

Did you know that...

Oviraptor *had only two teeth, turned downwards and growing from the palate; at first it was thought that these teeth were used to pierce the shells of the eggs of other animals.*
Then palaeontologists discovered fossilised eggs which still contained the embryos. The study of these eggs, very similar to those found in 1924 next to the skeleton of the first Oviraptor, *revealed that the embryos contained in the eggs belonged to* Oviraptor *itself. This dinosaur suddenly changed from being an eater of eggs to a loving parent.*

DINO QUIZ:

How is the existence of different kinds of skulls of *Oviraptor* explained?

Possibly the two kinds of skulls represent two different species of *Oviraptor*, or there may have been a difference between the male and female of the same species.

NOW, AS THEN ...

A skeleton of *Oviraptor* was discovered above a nest of eggs, in the same position that birds take when brooding their eggs.

PACHYCEPHALOSAURUS

NAME: *Pachycephalosaurus* means 'lizard with a thick head'.

DISCOVERED BY: Brown and Schlaikjer, in 1943.

CLASSIFICATION: Ornithischia, Marginocephalia, Pachycephalosauridae.

REMAINS: discovered in North America.

DIMENSIONS: length: 8 metres
weight: 2 tonnes.

FOOD: herbivore.

CHARACTERISTICS: *Pachycephalosaurus* was a dinosaur which lived in herds, was herbivorous, had small sharp teeth and walked on two rather stumpy legs. Its most distinctive feature was the armoured bony protection on top of its skull which it used against enemies and rivals. When attacking, it lowered its powerful head, held its body stretched forward, aligned parallel with the ground and its rigid tail horizontal. In addition it had protuberances and spikes both on its snout and around the osseous (bony) protection on the skull.

Did you know that...

Pachycephalosaurus had a very original armoured skull: an osseous (bony) cap, like a helmet, 25cm thick. Some scientists believe that it was a weapon used in fights. It is thought that during the mating season two male Pachycephalosauri would take a long run at each other and hit each other violently, using their heads as rams, or they might have wrestled, pushing their heads against each other to see who was the strongest. But more recent theories claim that the osseous cap on a Pachycephalosaurus was porous and fragile and served only to hold a crest or something similar when showing off in front of the females of the herd.

DINO QUIZ:

What kind of environment did *Pachycephalosaurus* live in?

It is most probable that *Pachycephalosaurus* lived in parts of North America which, about 70 million years ago, corresponded to the coastal regions

NOW, AS THEN ...

Male *Pachycephalosauri* fought as **rams** still do today: pushing their heads against each other to see which is the stronger.

PaCHYRHiNOSaURUS

NAME: *Pachyrhinosaurus* means 'lizard with the thick nose'.

DISCOVERED BY: C. M. Sternberg in 1950.

CLASSIFICATION: Ornithischia, Marginocephalia, Ceratopsidae.

REMAINS: discovered in North America.

DIMENSIONS: length: 6 metres
height: 2 metres.

FOOD: herbivore.

CHARACTERISTICS: *Pachyrhinosaurus* was a relative of the famous *Triceratops* but instead of real horns it had a curious, thick structure on its snout. It had an osseous (bony) collar round the neck with two spikes curved on the edges and a sort of horn in the centre. Along the middle line and the edges of the 'collar' were numerous little spikes. It was an herbivorous dinosaur with a beak to cut vegetation.
It walked on four stumpy legs and had a short tail.

Did you know that...

The remains of Pachyrhinosaurus, 12 partial skulls with many odd bones scattered around, were discovered in Alberta in Canada and in Alaska. It appears that this dinosaur lived and moved in large herds over thousands of kilometres and that its migrations took it to very high latitudes.

Some palaeontologists believe that the lump on the nose of *Pachyrhinosaurus* was the base of an enormous horn.

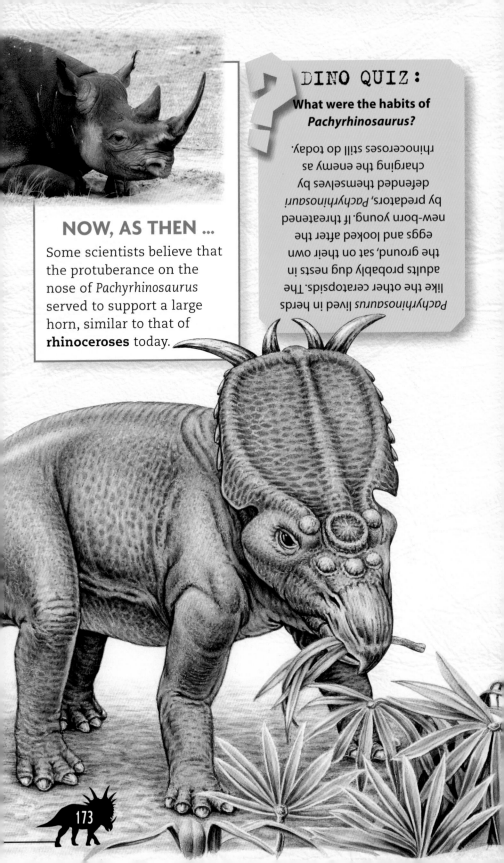

NOW, AS THEN ...

Some scientists believe that the protuberance on the nose of *Pachyrhinosaurus* served to support a large horn, similar to that of **rhinoceroses** today.

DINO QUIZ:

What were the habits of *Pachyrhinosaurus*?

Pachyrhinosaurus lived in herds like the other ceratopsids. The adults probably dug nests in the ground, sat on their own eggs and looked after the new-born young. If threatened by predators, *Pachyrhinosauri* defended themselves by charging the enemy as rhinoceroses still do today.

PARASAUROLOPHUS

NAME: *Parasaurolophus* means 'similar to a *Saurolophus*' and *Saurolophus* means 'lizard with the crest'.

DISCOVERED BY: Parks, in 1922.

CLASSIFICATION: Ornithischia, Ornithopoda, Hadrosauridae.

REMAINS: discovered in North America.

DIMENSIONS: length: 10 metres
height: 2.80 metres
weight: 2 tonnes.

FOOD: herbivore.

CHARACTERISTICS: *Parasaurolophus* was a herbivorous dinosaur with a duck's bill. It could walk on two or four legs. When it was grazing and eating low-growing plants it moved on four legs but when it was eating the leaves of tall trees it could stand on its hind legs. If threatened it could escape very quickly on two legs, keeping its tail well extended to balance the body.
It had a wide, flat snout and many serrated teeth, ideal for mincing and chewing tough plants.
It migrated in herds over long distances to look for food and to find safe places for getting together in colonies to make nests. It was able to look after its young and perhaps communicated by making sounds with the strange, elongated crest on top of its head.

Did you know that...

Parasaurolophus had a very strange head, adorned with a flamboyant, tubular bony crest pointing backwards which in some cases could reach a length of 1.80 metres. The crest was hollow inside and connected to the nose. Palaeontologists have long debated its function. Initially it was believed that it served either to increase its sense of smell or to breathe when the animal was under water, like a snorkel. But recent research indicates that the crest acted as a resonator to amplify the cries made by Parasaurolophus: sounds it emitted to identify itself and to communicate, songs to court females, calls for help and to warn its companions of approaching danger. The sounds must have had a very low frequency, similar to those of bass wind instruments and could have been heard from a long distance.

NOW, AS THEN ...

Reindeer and caribou have antlers or large horns on the top of the head. The antlers on the females are smaller than those of the males. Similarly the crests of the male and female *Parasaurolophus* differed in size. It is thought that the crests of the males, larger than those of the females, were brightly coloured and showy to attract the females.

DINO QUIZ:

Did *Parasaurolophus* young have a crest?

The young had no crest; it grew only as they got older and reached their full size with adulthood.

PARKSOSAURUS

NAME: *Parksosaurus* means 'Parks's lizard', after William Arthur Parks, the palaeontologist.

DISCOVERED BY: C. M. Sternberg, in 1937.

CLASSIFICATION: Ornithischia, Ornithopoda, Hypsilophodontidae.

REMAINS: discovered in North America.

DIMENSIONS: length: 2 metres
height: 1 metre.

FOOD: herbivore.

CHARACTERISTICS: *Parksosaurus* was a small herbivorous dinosaur which walked on two legs . It had short, powerful legs, a long tail, strong forelimbs and a long neck. Its head was small with an osseous beak. Its jaws were wide with very unusual teeth, short with rounded crests.

Did you know that...

Parksosaurus *was one of the fastest runners among dinosaurs and was one of the last survivors of a family of small, agile dinosaurs known as hypsilophodontids.*

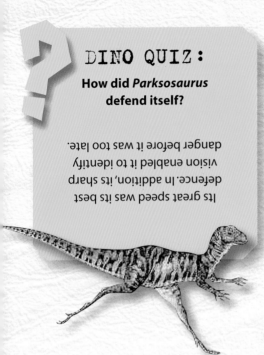

DINO QUIZ:

How did *Parksosaurus* defend itself?

Its great speed was its best defence. In addition, its sharp vision enabled it to identify danger before it was too late.

Past and Present

Originally *Parksosaurus* was called *Thescelosaurus* and classed in another group of ornithischian dinosaurs. But the differences in the rear limbs, for instance the appearance and joints of the claws, led scientists to class it in another genus. As a result it was renamed *Parksosaurus*, in honour of Canadian palaeontologist William Arthur Parks.

Pelecanimimus

NAME: *Pelecanimimus* means 'pelican mimic'.

DISCOVERED BY: Perez-Moreno, Sanz, Buscalioni, Moretalia, Ortega and Rasskin-Gutman, in 1994.

CLASSIFICATION: Saurischia, Theropoda, Ornithomimidae.

REMAINS: discovered in Europe.

DIMENSIONS: length: 2.5 metres.

FOOD: carnivore.

CHARACTERISTICS: *Pelecanimimus* was a bipedal carnivorous dinosaur and an agile, light and fast runner. It had a long, thin snout with over 200 teeth, more than any other known theropod. It had a crest on the back of its neck and possibly a pouch of skin at the front of its neck near its throat.

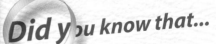

Did you know that...

Pelecanimimus *was the first ornithomimid discovered in Europe. Its fossil remains were discovered near Las Hoyas, an important palaeontological site situated in the Spanish province of Cienca.*

The palaeontological excavation in Las Hoyas, Spain.

? DINO QUIZ:

**What kind of
Pelecanimimus remains
have been discovered?**

Pelecanimimus is known from
the discovery of a skull, parts of
a skeleton and a few imprints of
muscles and skin.

NOW, AS THEN ...

The fossil remains of
Pelecanimimus reveal a
structure which is similar
to the pouch of today's
pelicans, used by them to
store the fish they catch.

PIATNITZKYSAURUS

NAME: *Piatnitzkysaurus* means 'Pianitzky's lizard', in honour of Alejandro Mateievich Piatnitzky, an Argentinian geologist of Russian origin who in 1936 discovered the fossil-rich Jurassic site of Cerro Condor in the Argentinian province of Chubut.

DISCOVERED BY: Bonaparte, in 1979.

CLASSIFICATION: Saurischia, Theropoda.

REMAINS: discovered in South America.

DIMENSIONS: length: 4.30 metres
height: 2.10 metres

FOOD: carnivore.

CHARACTERISTICS: *Piatnitzkysaurus* was a fairly solidly built carnivorous dinosaur, not particularly large, which walked on its hind legs. It had well-developed forelimbs, a powerful skull and long, pointed teeth, as sharp as knives.

Did you know that...

Piatnitzkysaurus has not yet been classed with absolute certainty: some palaeontologists believe that it is related to allosaurs, others believe that it is a primitive carnosaur, others again believe that it is a primitive tetanur, while yet others think it is an ancestor of the Abelisaurids.

DINO QUIZ:

What served as prey for *Pianitzkysaurus*?

Large primitive sauropod dinosaurs such as *Patagosaurus* may have been eaten by *Pianitzkysaurus*. Their fossil remains were discovered on the same site as those of the *Pianitzkysaurus*.

past and present

Pianitzkysaurus remains were discovered in the province of Chubut in the course of palaeontological expeditions organised by the Argentinian Museum of Natural History and led by the research scientist José Bonaparte in 1977, 1982 and 1983.

PLATEOSAURUS

NAME: *Plateosaurus* means 'flat lizard'.

DISCOVERED BY: von Meyer, in 1837.

CLASSIFICATION: Saurischia, Prosauropoda, Plateosauridae.

REMAINS: found in Europe, Africa, America, Asia, Australia.

DIMENSIONS: length: 8 metres
height: 5 metres
weight: 4 tonnes.

FOOD: herbivore.

CHARACTERISTICS: *Plateosaurus* had a long tail and long neck, a small head and a wide belly, probably to house the cumbersome bowels needed to digest the large quantities of plants it consumed. It mainly ate leaves which it tore off even the highest branches of trees, standing on its hind legs to do so. Given the shape of its sharply serrated teeth which were perfectly adapted for eating both plant matter and small prey, scientists do not exclude the possibility that *Plateosaurus* occasionally ate meat. Its powerful claws could be used to dig up roots or to defend itself against predators.
Normally *Plateosaurus* would walk on four legs but when faced with danger, it was capable of running like a biped and was probably faster than any other quadruped.

Did you know that...

Numerous Plateosaurus skeletons have been discovered together on the same site: a real cemetery which leads scientists to believe that they lived in large groups.

DINO QUIZ:

How many million years ago did *Plateosaurus* live?

Plateosaurus lived about 210 million years ago, towards the end of the Triassic period; it is one of the oldest dinosaurs in the world.

past and present

The wide geographic distribution of *Plateosaurus* is easily explained. In the Triassic period the Earth was one large continent and there were no oceans or mountain ranges to cross. Consequently, *Plateosaurus* could migrate all over the world.

The Earth during the Triassic period.

PROTOavis

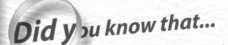

NAME: *Protoavis* means 'primitive bird'.

DISCOVERED BY: Chatterjee, in 1991.

CLASSIFICATION: Saurischia, Theropoda, Herrerasauridae.

REMAINS: discovered in North America.

DIMENSIONS: length: 30 centimetres.

FOOD: insectivore.

CHARACTERISTICS: *Protoavis* was a small, graceful bird dinosaur, more or less the same size as a pheasant. It had a narrow skull on an S-shaped neck, with small predator's teeth on the front part of its jaws which it used to eat insects, small animals and possibly fish. It had short front limbs and enormous hands. It moved with great agility, running on its hind legs and balancing on its tail. The structure of its claws suggests that *Protoavis* was able to climb trees.

Did you know that...

Protoavis was discovered in 1986 in Texas. The remains of its skeleton displayed characteristics which were typical of birds while other features were typical of dinosaurs. Some scientists therefore recognise it as the oldest ancestor of birds, while others believe it is a real dinosaur, placing it on the line of evolution which subsequently led to real birds. Given that there is only one skeleton in existence, it is probably wise not to draw any firm conclusions.

NOW, AS THEN ...

The eyes of *Protoavis* were placed frontally and were very large, like those of owls today – from which experts conclude that it hunted at dusk and night-time.

? **DINO QUIZ:**

Did *Protoavis* have feathers like *Archaeopteryx*?

Scientists are not certain but they have found signs on its remains which may indicate the presence of feathers.

PROTOCERATOPS

NAME: *Protoceratops* means 'First Horned face'.

DISCOVERED BY: Granger and Gregory, in 1923.

CLASSIFICATION: Ornithischia, Marginocephalia, Protoceratopsidae.

REMAINS: discovered in Asia.

DIMENSIONS: length: 2 metres
weight: 400 kilograms.

FOOD: herbivore.

CHARACTERISTICS: *Protoceratops* was a herbivorous dinosaur, a slow-moving quadruped with stumpy legs. It had a powerful, cumbersome body, a short, thick tail, a large head with a parrot's beak to cut plants — and teeth at the back of its mouth to chew them. The males had a larger frill than the females, suggesting that this frill probably played a part in the animal's courtship.

Did you know that...

Protoceratops *was probably an animal which lived in a herd, like the other ceratopsids related to it. This hypothesis is supported by the discovery of vast numbers of their fossil remains on the same site and the presence of numerous nests.* Protoceratops *laid 12 or more eggs in each nest, arranging them in a spiral.*

What was the purpose of the frill round *Protoceratops's* neck?

The neck frill served to protect the neck, to anchor the jaw muscles and possibly also to impress others.

past and present

Protoceratops remains were discovered in the Gobi desert in Mongolia.

In 1971 some particularly interesting remains were discovered, clinging to the skeleton of *Velociraptor*. It is believed that the two dinosaurs died fighting, surprised by a sandstorm which struck suddenly.

Scientists have discovered many nests – and fossilised eggs that contain embryos of *Protoceratops*.

The reconstructed skeleton of *Protoceratops* shown near a nest.

187

PSITTACOSAURUS

NAME: *Psittacosaurus* means 'Parrot lizard'.

DISCOVERED BY: Osborn, in 1923.

CLASSIFICATION: Ornithischia, Marginocephalia, Psittacosauridae.

REMAINS: discovered in Asia.

DIMENSIONS: length: 2 metres
height: 1.20 metres
weight: 80 kilograms

FOOD: herbivore.

CHARACTERISTICS: *Psittacosaurus* was a herbivorous dinosaur. Its beak was osseous (bony), powerful and curved like that of a parrot, ideal for tearing apart plants and vegetation. At the back of its mouth it had teeth which enabled it to chew its food. Its skull was short and its hind legs much longer than its front limbs that had hands with four long digits.

Did you know that...

Psittacosaurus was a small primitive ceratopsid, fast-moving thanks to its long hind legs. Its short, compact skull was fitted with a beak like that of a parrot.

The long digits on its hands enabled *Psittacosaurus* to grab hold of branches and leaves.

DINO QUIZ:

Have there been any recent surprising discoveries regarding *Psittacosaurus*?

Recently, scientists have made a surprising discovery: a *Psittacosaurus* with structures on its tail resembling long feathers. Another more recent discovery shows thin, feathery filaments on its back.

past and present

Psittacosaurus was one of the most widespread dinosaurs in the Cretaceous period. Its fossilised remains have been found all over Asia: in Japan, Siberia, Mongolia, China and Thailand.

The beak of the *Psittacosaurus* was powerful, short and curved — very similar to that of a parrot.

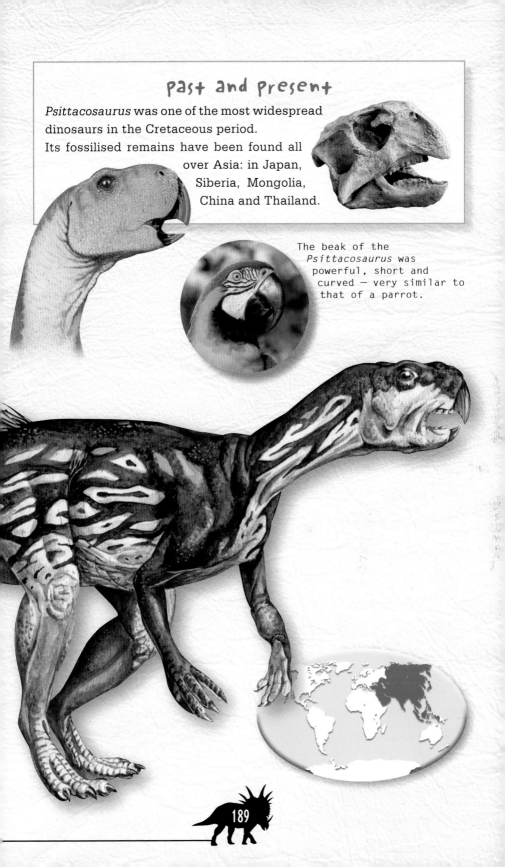

Quaesitosaurus

NAME: *Quaesitosaurus* means 'extraordinary lizard'.

DISCOVERED BY: Kurzanov and Bannikov, in 1983.

CLASSIFICATION: Saurischia, Sauropoda, Nemegtosauridae.

REMAINS: discovered in Asia.

DIMENSIONS: length: 23 metres.

FOOD: herbivore.

CHARACTERISTICS: *Quaesitosaurus* had a gigantic belly to hold all the food which it ingested, a long tail which provided a counterweight to its long neck, four massive, columnar legs and a very small forehead compared to its body and its wide snout.

Did you know that...

The skull of Quaesitosaurus was very unusual: it was elongated with a wide snout and wide openings for the ears. The teeth were like sharp spikes and this suggests that it ate tender plants, perhaps including some aquatic plants.

190

DINO QUIZ:

Why did large sauropods like *Quaesitosaurus* have such long necks?

The sauropod usually had a very long neck, more or less parallel to the ground, with which it foraged through the branches and leaves of tall trees that it would otherwise have been unable to reach, because of its bulky body.

Past and Present

Quaesitosaurus is known only from fragments of skull discovered in the Gobi desert. This environment was semi-arid during the Mesozoic period.

191

SALTRIOSAURUS

latest discovery

NAME: *Saltriosaurus* means 'Saltrio's lizard', named after the place in Italy near which it was discovered: Saltrio, in the province of Varese.

DISCOVERED BY: Dal Sasso, in 2001.

CLASSIFICATION: Saurischia, Tetanurae.

REMAINS: discovered in Europe

DIMENSIONS: length: 8 metres
height: 4 metres
weight: 1.5 tonnes.

FOOD: carnivore.

CHARACTERISTICS: *Saltriosaurus* was a biped predator which relied on its long, rigid tail for balance. It had a gigantic skull, about 70 centimetres long and enormous sharp teeth. The arms were well-developed and the hands had fingers, ending in powerful claws. *Saltriosaurus* is only known through a few remains of bones. One of these, a forked bone called a furcula, formed by the fusion of the two clavicles, is of particular interest to palaeontologists because, having a delicate structure, it is rare.

Did you know that...

Saltriosaurus *is the largest carnivorous dinosaur discovered in Italy. It lived at the beginning of the Jurassic period, about 200 million years ago. With its three-fingered hands and rigid tail, it is one of the oldest tetanor dinosaurs.*

DINO QUIZ:

What is the furcula of a *Saltriosaurus* and why is it so important?

The furcula is a forked bone like a wishbone, formed by the fusion of two clavicles, found in birds and in theropod dinosaurs. It used to be believed typical of birds and the group of dinosaurs from which birds descended. However, scientists now know that many other dinosaurs had this bone.

past and present

The scientific study of *Saltriosaurus* has not been completed so no formal published description exists yet. In addition, *Saltriosaurus* is a '*nomen nudum*', a temporary name, given to the dinosaur in 1996 at the time it was discovered.

SAUROLOPHUS

NAME: *Saurolophus* means 'lizard with the crest'.

DISCOVERED BY: Brown, in 1912.

CLASSIFICATION: Ornithischia, Ornithopoda, Hadrosauridae.

REMAINS: found in North America and Asia.

DIMENSIONS: length: 12 metres.

FOOD: herbivore.

CHARACTERISTICS: *Saurolophus* was a biped dinosaur with a duck's bill; it could also walk on four legs, especially when browsing on low vegetation. It had a massive body, a long tail, front limbs shorter than the hind legs, the digits ending in small hoofs, a flattened head with an elongated crest pointing backwards and a beak without teeth. Inside its mouth were hundreds of teeth arranged in rows.

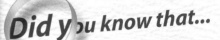

Did you know that...

Saurolophus *had a very unusual crest on its head which extended towards and beyond the back of the skull. It had a pointed end like a horn. In addition, it had a bony ring round the eyes, a feature found in no other duck-billed dinosaur.*

past and present

The *Saurolophus* genus disappeared during the great crisis which hit our planet in the Cretaceous period, leading to the extinction of many dinosaurs and countless other groups of living creatures.

What was the purpose of the crest of the *Saurolophus*?

The function of the crest is not known with certainty. It was a solid bone which was an extension of the nose bone. Some palaeontologists have suggested that it may have served to support a bag of skin (placed above the nose) which could be inflated to emit powerful sounds.

The lower and upper jaw were very wide and flattened. This made the snout of *Saurolophus* look like a duck's bill.

195

SAUROPELTA

NAME: *Sauropelta* means 'lizard shield'.

DISCOVERED BY: Ostrom, in 1970.

CLASSIFICATION: Ornithischia, Thyreophora, Nodosauridae.

REMAINS: discovered in North America.

DIMENSIONS: length: 7.5 metres
weight: 3 tonnes.

FOOD: herbivore.

CHARACTERISTICS: *Sauropelta* was an armoured quadruped dinosaur which fed on plants. Slow, fat and heavy, it had a rather narrow skull with strong jaws, with small, sharp teeth and an osseous beak with teeth. Its armour which protected the back, the head and long tail from predators. In addition, it had a long row of bony spikes along the sides.

Did you know that...

The thick armour which covered Sauropelta's body consisted of osseous nodules and scutes (shield-like plates), embedded in the skin which was very tough as a result. These nodules and scutes extended along the entire back and tail, forming an armour which protected parts of the body most exposed to the bites of predators. It had a row of long, very dangerous spikes along each side; these pointed outwards and provided further protection.

past and present

The remains of a *Sauropelta* were discovered in Cloverly Formation in Montana. It was an almost complete and well-preserved skeleton — which showed details of both the armour and the bones of the animal. It was described by the palaeontologist John Ostrom in 1970 and is now exhibited at the American Museum of Natural History in New York.

DINO QUIZ:

From which dinosaurs did *Sauropelta* have to defend itself?

Deinonychus and *Albertosaurus* were among the potential predators against which *Sauropelta* might have had to defend itself.

197

SaUROPOSEIDON

NAME: *Sauroposeidon* means 'Poseidon lizard', after the name of the Greek god of the sea.

DISCOVERED BY: Wedel, Cifelli and Sanders, in 2000.

CLASSIFICATION: Saurischia, Sauropoda, Brachiosauridae.

REMAINS: discovered in North America.

DIMENSIONS: length: 28 metres
height: 18 metres
weight: 60 tonnes.

FOOD: herbivore.

CHARACTERISTICS: With its short body, graceful but extremely long neck and the forelimbs longer than its hind legs, *Sauroposeidon* had a giraffe-like appearance. It is thought that this enormous sauropod used its very long neck and remarkable height to reach the best shoots and branches at the top of the tallest trees. It is possible that the bones of *Sauroposeidon*, like those of other large sauropods, were honeycombed with pockets of air to reduce body weight. It is thought that an adult *Sauroposeidon* which weighed about 60 tons probably had no enemies capable of attacking it.

Did you know that...

The only remains of Sauroposeidon *known* today are four cervical vertebrae. The size of these bones has enabled scientists to calculate the size of the animal: it reached a height of about 18 metres, by far the tallest dinosaur known!

past and present

The four cervical vertebrae of *Sauroposeidon* were discovered in 1994, in sediments in the Antlers Formation in Oklahoma, by the palaeontologist Richard Cifelli and a team of research scientists from the Oklahoma Museum of Natural History. In 1999, Dr Cifelli asked the student Matt Wedel to examine these vertebrae. The result of his analysis was surprising: the vertebrae belonged to a dinosaur about 18 metres tall! In October 1999, this news was announced publicly and, in March 2000, an official article appeared in the *Journal of Vertebrate Paleontology*.

DINO QUIZ:

How long was the neck of *Sauroposeidon*?

The neck of *Sauroposeidon* is thought to have been about 12 metres long.

199

JURASSIC
SCELIDOSAURUS

NAME: *Scelidosaurus* means 'limb lizard'.

DISCOVERED BY: Owen, in 1859.

CLASSIFICATION: Ornithischia, Thyreophora, Scelidosauridae?

REMAINS: discovered in Europe, North America and Asia.

DIMENSIONS: length: 4 metres
weight: 250 kilograms.

FOOD: herbivore.

CHARACTERISTICS: *Scelidosaurus* was a quadruped dinosaur with powerful hind legs and shorter, slender fore limbs. Its tapered body was long and low, its head was small on a short neck and its tail was long and rigid. It had small osseous plates or scutes embedded in the skin which covered and protected the back, neck, tail and perhaps the sides as well. It had three small pointed horns behind the auditory cavities. The teeth, serrated like the edges of a leaf but rather small, indicate that *Scelidosaurus* fed mainly on leaves which it just swallowed because it had no chewing ability; a boney beak on its nose may have helped to tear the vegetation.

Did you know that...

Scelidosaurus seems too primitive to be classed in either of the two groups of known armoured dinosaurs: stegosaurs and ankylosaurs. Some palaeontologists see it as a primitive stegosaur because of certain skull features while others believe it is a primitive ankylosaur with the beginnings of armour; yet other scientists place Scelidosaurus in a group of little-evolved dinosaurs, together with Scutellosaurus. Perhaps Scelidosaurus or one of its direct descendants is the ancestor of the ankylosaurs or stegosaurs.

DINO QUIZ:

How many millions of years ago did *Scelidosaurus* live?

Scelidosaurus lived in the Lower Jurassic period, between 200 and 206 million years ago.

Past and Present

The first fossils of *Scelidosaurus* were discovered in England in 1859. The incomplete skeleton was found in a quarry in cliffs near the sea; it was therefore thought that *Scelidosaurus* was an aquatic lizard.

In 1955 a second, (and more complete) skeleton was discovered, enabling scientists to realise their mistake: *Scelidosaurus* was not an aquatic lizard but a dinosaur.

SCIPIONYX

NAME: The name *Scipionyx* means 'Scipione's claw' in honour of the geologist Scipione Breislack who, in 1798, was the first to discover the existence of fossils in Pietraroja, Benevento, Italy, where this discovery was made. *Scipionyx* is better known by its informal nickname 'Skippy'.

DISCOVERED BY: Todesco in 1998 and named by Dal Sasso and Signore.

CLASSIFICATION: Saurischia, Theropoda, Coelurosauria.

REMAINS: discovered in Europe.

DIMENSIONS: length: 50 centimetres.

FOOD: carnivore.

CHARACTERISTICS: *Scipionyx* was a young specimen of a dinosaur genus which would have reached two metres as an adult. It was a fast-running biped dinosaur. Its anatomy is reminiscent of that of a *Velociraptor*, even though the two genuses are not part of the same family. It had numerous sharp teeth and hands with three digits ending in sharp and powerful claws; it had a long tail to help it maintain its balance. It is believed that it hunted and ate small vertebrates and insects.

Did you know that...

Scipionyx was the first dinosaur discovered in Italy. It was found by Giovanni Todesco, an enthusiastic amateur palaeontologist, near Pietraroja, Benevento, in southern Italy. It was an incredible discovery: a juvenile carnivorous dinosaur which lived at the beginning of the Cretaceous period. The skeleton was well preserved with the bones in perfect anatomical connection and almost complete, missing only the tail and part of the hind legs. Scipionyx, nicknamed 'Skippy', is known throughout the world because it still has some of its internal organs which is seldom the case with fossils.

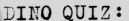

Past and Present

In the Lower Cretaceous period
the locality of **Pietraroja** was a
small lagoon of shallow waters,
a warm and peaceful place.

SINRAPTOR

NAME: *Sinraptor* means 'Chinese predator'.

DISCOVERED BY: Currie and Zhao, in 1994.

CLASSIFICATION: Saurischia, Theropoda, Sinraptoridae.

REMAINS: discovered in China.

DIMENSIONS: length: 7 metres.

FOOD: carnivore.

CHARACTERISTICS: *Sinraptor* was a carnosaur with an enormous head. Its sharp teeth were serrated along the edges and curved inwards. This biped dinosaur had a slender body and two long hind legs. Its front limbs had three digits with claws.

Did you know that...

The discovery of Sinraptor provided scientists with further data that helped them to understand the relationship that existed between the carnivorous dinosaurs in the group of carnosaurs. It should be pointed out that Sinraptor, a fairly small carnosaur, might be the ancestor of the larger Giganotosaurus and Carcharodontosaurus and was also a possible ancestor of the allosaurs.

204

SPINOSAURUS

NAME: *Spinosaurus* means 'spine lizard', so named because of the long spines on its back which were probably connected by skin to form a sail-like structure.

DISCOVERED BY: Stromer, in 1915.

CLASSIFICATION: Saurischia, Theropoda, Spinosauridae.

REMAINS: discovered in North Africa.

DIMENSIONS: length: 17 metres
weight: 9 tonnes.

FOOD: carnivore and piscivore.

CHARACTERISTICS: *Spinosaurus* was a large carnivorous dinosaur with an enormous skull, nearly 2 metres long, the thin, elongated shape of which is very reminiscent of a crocodile. It had powerful jaws and terrifying teeth which were conical and pointed, more like those of a crocodile than those of other dinosaurs. This particular feature led scientists to believe that it fed mainly on large fish. It was a biped dinosaur which, considering its size, was agile and light-footed. Its front limbs were well developed and shaped to grab prey while the tail was rigid and tapered to provide the necessary balance while moving.

Did you know that...

Spinosaurus *was much larger than the famous Tyrannosaurus!*
The large sail-like structure on its back gave it a majestic appearance. Some scientists believe that this structure helped regulate the animal's body temperature: exposed to the sun, it quickly absorbed heat which spread throughout the body via the circulation of the blood. The sail would have enabled it to get rid of excess body heat and so avoid overheating.

DINO QUIZ:

How large was the dorsal sail of *Spinosaurus*?

Some of the neural spines discovered have been as long as 1.80 metres: as tall as an adult man!

NOW, AS THEN ...

Some scientists believe that the sail-like structure of *Spinosaurus* was brightly coloured and was used to intimidate other males or as a sexual display during the mating season.

Today males of many animal and bird species also have showy, colourful structures which they use for these purposes.

STAURIKOSAURUS

NAME: The name *Staurikosaurus* or 'Lizard of the Southern Cross' was inspired by a constellation of the southern hemisphere which shone in the night sky in prehistoric times just as it does today.

DISCOVERED BY: Colbert, in 1970.

CLASSIFICATION: Saurischia, Theropoda.

REMAINS: discovered in South America.

DIMENSIONS: length: 1.80 metres
height: 80 centimetres
weight: 30 kilograms.

FOOD: carnivore.

CHARACTERISTICS: *Staurikosaurus* was a primitive dinosaur. It was a biped with long hind legs. It was a very fast runner and a terrifying hunter. Thanks to its agility and its light body structure, it was able to bring down prey much larger than itself. Its short forelimbs ended in primitive five-digit hands. The body was elongated with a long flexible tail.

Did you know that...

Staurikosaurus could be the ancestor of the dinosaurs! It is one of the most primitive of all known dinosaurs and, according to scientists, it does not fit properly into either the group of the prosauropods (the dinosaurs which developed into the gigantic herbivorous sauropods), or that of the celurosauri (the small carnivorous dinosaurs such as Coelophysis and Procompsognathus).

past and present

Only a single fossil specimen of *Staurikosaurus* exists and this was discovered in the sediments of the Santa Maria Formation in the Rio Grande de Sul in Brazil.

The discovery was made in the 1970s and is very incomplete; it consists only of parts of the spinal column, legs and jaw.

DINO QUIZ:

From which lizards did the dinosaurs evolve?

In the Triassic period the Earth was swarming with lizards. These included the thecodonts which were particularly well evolved with almost completely straight legs and strong teeth, deeply anchored into the jawbone. Dinosaurs probably developed from the thecodonts.

STEGOSAURUS

NAME: *Stegosaurus*, the 'roof lizard' was so called because of the array of tile-like triangular plates on its back.

DISCOVERED BY: O. C. Marsh, in 1877.

CLASSIFICATION: Ornithischia, Thyreophora, Stegosauridae.

REMAINS: discovered in North America.

DIMENSIONS: length: 9 metres
height: 4 metres
weight: 2 tonnes.

FOOD: herbivore.

CHARACTERISTICS: *Stegosaurus* was the largest representative of the family of stegosaurs. It had a very small head, a large body and front limbs shorter than the hind legs. Its distinctive feature was the presence of 17 plates on its back, some as high as one metre, leaf-like in shape and arranged in two rows. At the extremity of the sturdy tail were two pairs of spikes and round the neck it had numerous small plates to protect its throat from the bites of predators. *Stegosaurus* was a quadruped dinosaur which wandered through woodland clearings, peacefully browsing on the plants and vegetation, proudly displaying the crest adorning its back. The sharp spikes on its tail were its main weapons of defence.

Did you know that...

Stegosaurus is one of the most famous dinosaurs but perhaps not everyone knows that the characteristic plates on its back did not have a defensive role. The hypothesis that they were defensive structures was rejected by palaeontologists when it was discovered that these plates contained numerous blood vessels, meaning that in the event of injury, it would have bled abundantly, thus putting the animal in serious danger. Instead it is now thought that the plates controlled body heat. To get warm, *Stegosaurus* would position itself where the rays of the sun hit the plates; the blood inside would warm up and then flow through the rest of the body, thus raising the body temperature. If, on the other hand, the animal overheated, the plates could quickly get rid of any excess heat.

? DINO QUIZ:

Is it true that *Stegosaurus* had more than one brain?

Stegosaurus had a very small brain in its skull, weighing about 70 grams but there were other nervous ganglions or small 'additional brains' placed at various points along the bone marrow which served to accelerate the speed at which nervous impulses were transmitted. Thanks to this system, *Stegosaurus* was able to control the movements of its legs and tail better.

Past and Present

Over the years, palaeontologists have developed a variety of theories on the arrangement of the plates on the back of *Stegosaurus*. According to some they were positioned vertically in two parallel rows, while according to others they were horizontal and formed a kind of roof on the back of the animal. Today scientists believe that the plates were arranged in two rows but staggered so as to capture the rays of the sun better and halfway down the back they formed a single row.

211

STRUTHIOMIMUS

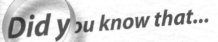

NAME: *Struthiomimus* means 'ostrich imitator'.

DISCOVERED BY: Osborn, in 1916.

CLASSIFICATION: Saurischia, Theropoda, Ornithomimidae.

REMAINS: discovered in North America.

DIMENSIONS: length: 3.5 metres
height: 2 metres
weight: 300 kilograms.

FOOD: omnivore.

CHARACTERISTICS: *Struthiomimus* was a biped dinosaur with an agile, light skeleton and four long, slender legs. It was very similar to an ostrich of today with arms instead of wings and no feathers.
It had a stocky body but a long neck and a long tail. The head was small with a toothless osseous beak, ideal for capturing insects and small lizards or for picking up grains and vegetation of all kinds, assisted by its long arms and hands with three digits, perfect for picking up and catching prey.
It had large eyes which gave it excellent vision. Given the considerable size of its cranium, palaeontologists believe that this was one of the most intelligent dinosaurs.

Did you know that...

With its long, slender hind legs, Struthiomimus was able to run incredibly fast, touching 50 kilometres an hour and the curved claws on its toes gave it an excellent grip on the ground. In case of danger, flight was its only defence: it lived in the open countryside where running fast was the only way to escape to safety. Its speciality was sprint-racing and it was certainly good at it!

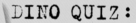

DINO QUIZ:

Did *Struthiomimus* live alone or in a group?

Struthiomimus had no particular means of defence except speed; it is therefore possible that it lived in a group to benefit from the protection of companions and to increase the chances of seeing a predator in time to make an escape.

NOW, AS THEN ...

The size and appearance of *Struthiomimus* are reminiscent of **ostriches** today. Like them it was an omnivore and could run incredibly fast.

A *Struthiomimus* toe claw.

STYRACOSAURUS

NAME: The name *Styracosaurus* means 'spiked lizard' and referred to the many pointed spines and horns framing its head.

DISCOVERED BY: Lambe, in 1913.

CLASSIFICATION: Ornithischia, Marginocephalia, Ceratopsidae.

REMAINS: discovered in North America.

DIMENSIONS: length: 5 metres
height: 2.5 metres
weight: 3 tonnes.

FOOD: herbivore.

CHARACTERISTICS: *Styracosaurus* was a quadruped with four short, stocky legs. It had a large skull which ended in a parrot's beak – used to cut the vegetation and plants it ate. It had an osseous frill round its neck from which six spikes protruded plus a horn on its nose and two small ones near its eyes. The tail was short and thick and the body bulky and cumbersome.

Did you know that...

The distinctive feature of Styracosaurus was the osseous frill, adorned with six long, pointed spikes and other smaller ones along the edge of this frill, a 60 cm long horn on its nose and two small horns near the eyes. This armoured head must have been an effective deterrent against predators and was used in encounters between males of the species.

The bony frill of *Styracosaurus* was surrounded by long spikes.

DINO QUIZ:

What was the purpose of the osseous collar of *Styracosaurus*?

The collar protected the shoulders, back and neck and provided an excellent anchorage for powerful masticatory muscles; some scientists believe that it was also brightly coloured to attract females.

NOW, AS THEN ...

Numerous fossil remains of Styracosaurus have been found in Alberta in Canada and they have all been found close to each other in deposits known as 'bone beds'. Possibly the large herds of Styracosaurus crossed rivers during their migrations and many drowned because of the strong currents. The drowning of an entire herd of **herbivorous mammals** was rather more frequent then than it is now.

SUCHOMIMUS

Latest discovery

NAME: *Suchomimus* means 'crocodile mimic'.

DISCOVERED BY: Sereno, Beck, Dutheil, Gado, Larsson, Lyon, Marcot, Rauhut, Sadleir, Sidor, Varricchio, G. P. Wilson and J. A. Wilson, in 1998.

CLASSIFICATION: Saurischia, Theropoda, Spinosauridae.

REMAINS: discovered in north-west Africa.

DIMENSIONS: length: 11 metres
height: 3.60 metres.

FOOD: carnivore and piscivore.

CHARACTERISTICS: *Suchomimus* was a carnivorous dinosaur with a crocodile-like skull: elongated with a small osseous crest at the top and narrow jaws with about a hundred sharp teeth, curved slightly backwards. This was almost double the number usually present in the mouth of other theropods. The front limbs ended in three digits with claws. The first digit of each hand had a claw 40 centimetres long. On the back the vertebrae were elongated and covered with skin to form a kind of sail or flap.

Did you know that...

The structure of the skull of Suchomimus was adapted to catch fish and suggests that it lived and fed in the same way that crocodiles do today. From the banks of rivers it harpooned fish with its claws and held onto them with its long snout and numerous curved teeth.

The skull and front leg of *Suchomimus*.

216

Did the skeleton of *Suchomimus* discovered in 1998 belong to an adult?

No, the remains which have been discovered belonged to an animal not yet fully developed; this means that an adult *Suchomimus* would have been even bigger.

Past and Present

Suchomimus was discovered in Niger in the Sahara desert by a team of research scientists led by the palaeontologist Paul Sereno. It lived about 110 million years ago when the Sahara was a green plain, covered with vegetation. It was described in 1998 by Paul Sereno and other palaeontologist colleagues on the basis of a single skeleton, about 70% complete. Its remains were very similar to those of an English dinosaur, *Baryonyx*, so much so that some scientists doubted the existence of the *Suchomimus* as a genus and included it in *Baryonyx*.

SUPERSAURUS

NAME: *Supersaurus* means 'super lizard'.

DISCOVERED BY: Jensen, in 1985.

CLASSIFICATION: Saurischia, Sauropoda, Diplodocidae.

REMAINS: discovered in North America.

DIMENSIONS: length: 42 metres
height: 16.5 metres
weight: 30 to 50 tonnes
approx.

FOOD: herbivore.

CHARACTERISTICS: *Supersaurus* was an enormous dinosaur which moved on four stocky, columnar legs. Its front limbs were shorter than the back legs. Its neck was 12 metres long and *Supersaurus* could probably move it to the right and to the left, although its vertical mobility was probably rather restricted. The head was very small and the jaws studded with pencil-shaped teeth. The tail was long to provide a counterweight to the weight of the long neck and became thinner towards the end like a whip. To control it and use it with precision, *Supersaurus* had a thickening of the spinal cord, at the level of the hips, which acted as an additional 'brain'. The main weapon of this dinosaur, apart from its size, was its tail which it used as lethal whip; in addition it also had two claws on each thumb. *Supersaurus* moved in large herds, always in search of new pastures. Some of its eggs have been found in rows in a line as if they had been laid while the animal was walking; this suggests that *Supersaurus* did not sit on its own eggs or look after its young.

Did you know that...

At more than 40 metres long, Supersaurus was one of the longest animals that ever lived on Earth. This gigantic dinosaur lived at the end of the Jurassic period, the age of enormous sauropods such as Apatosaurus and Brachiosaurus.

Past and Present

When it was discovered in Colorado in the late 1970s, *Supersaurus* was believed to be related to the great *Brachiosaurus*. Then thanks to further discoveries and research, the genus was classed in the family of the diplodocids, characterised by their long necks.

The entrance to the Dinosaur National Museum in Colorado and Utah.

ENTERING **DINOSAUR** NATIONAL MONUMENT
UNITED STATES
DEPARTMENT OF THE INTERIOR
NATIONAL PARK SERVICE

The giant turtles of the Galapagos archipelago can live up to 170 years of age.

SYNOSAUROPTERYX

latest discovery

NAME: *Synosauropteryx* means 'Chinese lizard-wing'.

DISCOVERED BY: farmer Li Yinfang in 1996 and described by Ji Qiang.

CLASSIFICATION: Saurischia, Theropoda, Compsognathidae.

REMAINS: discovered in China.

DIMENSIONS: length: 1.25 metres
weight: 10 kilograms.

FOOD: carnivore.

CHARACTERISTICS: *Synosauropteryx* was a very fast biped runner, about the same size as a turkey, with a long tail. Its small, sharp teeth tell us that it was a carnivore. In size and dimension, it was very similar to *Compsognathus*. Its discovery in 1996 demonstrated that, in addition to certain similarities in their skeletons, dinosaurs and birds also shared the presentation of feathers. The fossil remains of *Sinosauropteryx* reveal vestiges of miniscule structures similar to rudimentary feathers, simple elongated filaments which seem to grow from the skin on the back, head and tail; this is probably what remains of a soft, warm, dense plumage which is thought to have covered the entire body of the animal. The feathers did not enable the animal to fly but helped to maintain its body temperature at the correct level. The fact that this was necessary shows that dinosaurs, at least the small, light ones, were warm-blooded animals.

Did you know that...

The discovery of feathered dinosaurs such as Synosauropteryx has triggered heated discussions among scientists: many of them believe that the small carnivorous feathered dinosaurs are the direct ancestors of birds.

Synosauropteryx was the same size as a turkey

DINO QUIZ:

What did
Synosauropteryx eat?

Synosauropteryx fed on small vertebrates, including mammals: the stomach of one of the specimens of *Synosauropteryx* still contains the jaws of *Zhangheotherium*, a small primitive mammal, similar to a **shrew.**

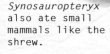

Synosauropteryx also ate small mammals like the shrew.

past and present

Synosauropteryx was discovered in the Liaoning province of north-east China, a few hundred kilometres from Beijing. In the Cretaceous period the province of Liaoning was a lush tropical forest, punctuated here and there by a few shallow lakes on the shores of which life thrived. Nearby were volcanoes which erupted now and again, spewing out lava. Streams of lava and tons of ashes covered the surrounding area, causing death all around. Many carcasses of the dead animals ended up in the lakes and were buried in sediment.

At the bottom of these Chinese lakes some feathered dinosaurs became fossilised and remained concealed for 120 million years until they were discovered by accident by some farmers.

SYNTARSUS

NAME: *Syntarsus* means 'fused tarsus'. The tarsus is a bone in the foot which is between the metatarsi – the bones which support the first phalanges of the fingers or toes – and the ankle.

DISCOVERED BY: Raath, in 1969.

CLASSIFICATION: Saurischia, Theropoda, Coelophysidae.

REMAINS: discovered in South Africa and North America.

DIMENSIONS: length: 3 metres
height: 1 metre
weight: 30 kilograms.

FOOD: carnivore.

CHARACTERISTICS: *Syntarsus* was a small, biped dinosaur which could run fast on its long, slender hind legs; it had hollow bones which made its skeleton much lighter.
Its skull was elongated, the neck S-shaped, the tail long and its hands and feet ended in four digits. It is probable that *Syntarsus* was covered in feathers, not to fly but to keep its body temperature constant.

Did you know that...

Syntarsus had a distinctive double crest on its skull, similar to that of Dilophosaurus. Scientists believe this was only for display.

Past and present

Many fossil remains of *Syntarsus* have been found in Zimbabwe in Africa and in Arizona in the United States. Some 30 skeletons have been discovered on the same site in Zimbabwe, suggesting that these small predators lived and hunted in groups.

DINO QUIZ:

How did *Syntarsus* move?

It may have run fast but some scientists think it hopped like a rabbit or kangaroo.

TARBOSAURUS

NAME: *Tarbosaurus* means 'terrifying lizard', because its size probably instilled fear in other animals.

DISCOVERED BY: Maleev, in 1955.

CLASSIFICATION: Saurischia, Theropoda, Tyrannosauridae.

REMAINS: discovered in Asia.

DIMENSIONS: length: 12 metres
height: 6 metres
weight: 4.5 tonnes.

FOOD: carnivore.

CHARACTERISTICS: *Tarbosaurus* was an enormous biped dinosaur with long, powerful hind legs. Its feet had three digits with claws, well-developed and facing forward and a small fourth finger facing backward. The length of some of the bones in its hind legs leads scientists to believe that *Tarbosaurus* was a rather fast runner. Its skull was gigantic, reaching up to 1.70 metres in length and its jaws were lined with 50 or so teeth which were long and curved. Its jaws were wide and powerful, capable of breaking the bones of its prey in a single bite. Its fore limbs were very short and the hands had two complete digits, each with a powerful claw and a third incomplete digit; palaeontologists do not know what role these forelimbs served because they were too short even to reach its mouth.

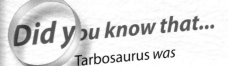

Did you know that...

Tarbosaurus was very similar to a Tyrannosaurus, so much so that some scientists believe the two could be the same animal. If this were true, Tarbosaurus would not be a valid scientific name and would be changed: Tyrannosaurs would become two species, Tyrannosaurus bataar and Tyrannosaurus efremovi. But all the remains of Tarbosaurus have been discovered in Mongolia while all Tyrannosaurus remains have been discovered in Canada,

thousands of kilometres away; it would therefore be strange if they were the same species. In addition, there are some anatomical differences between the two dinosaurs; Tarbosaurus, for instance, has a larger head and more slender body than Tyrannosaurus.

? DINO QUIZ:

How did
Tarbosaurus **hunt?**

Some scientists believe that
Tarbosaurus was an intelligent
hunter, capable of laying
ambushes and pursuing pre-
selected prey with great skill.
Other scientists, on the other hand,
think that because of its enormous
bulk, *Tarbosaurus* moved very
slowly and could eat only the
remains of dead animals or prey
taken from other dinosaurs.

Past and Present

The first fossil remains of *Tarbosaurus* were discovered in 1955 in Mongolia during the Russian expedition led by palaeontologist Maleev, who named the animal.

The Gobi desert in Mongolia.

225

TenonTosaurus

NAME: *Tenontosaurus* means 'sinew lizard'.

DISCOVERED BY: Ostrom, in 1970.

CLASSIFICATION: Ornithischia, Ornithopoda, (Iguanodontidae?)

REMAINS: discovered in North America

DIMENSIONS: length: 8 metres
weight: 1 tonne.

FOOD: herbivore.

CHARACTERISTICS: *Tenontosaurus* was a quadruped dinosaur, very big, bulky and cumbersome. It was heavy and muscular with a rather long neck and a very long tail. Its head displayed some primitive characteristics; the snout was long and the teeth flattened, not organised in rows and sophisticated like those of hadrosaurs but nevertheless efficient and capable of cutting and chewing vegetation.
It is thought that *Tenontosaurus* ran on two legs because its front legs were a little shorter than the hind legs and also that it spent most of its time grazing. Some scientists believe it to be a very large hypsolophodon, in contrast to the small, agile forms which lived in the Jurassic period. However, recent studies suggest that *Tenontosaurus* belongs instead to the family of iguanodons; in this case it would be one of the most primitive representatives of the group.

Did you know that...

In Montana fossil remains of Tenontosaurus were discovered together with several skeletons of Deinonychus.
Because Deinonychus was a predator and Tenontosaurus a herbivore and therefore a potential prey, it is possible that this discovery has revealed a hunting scene which became fossilised in time.

past and present

Today we know of two species of *Tenontosaurus: Tenontosaurus tillettorum*, the type species, discovered in Montana and *Tenontosaurus dossi*, the species characteristic of Texas.

THERIZINOSAURUS

NAME: *Therizinosaurus* or 'claw lizard' was so named because of the incredibly long claw-like nails on the digits of its hands.

DISCOVERED BY: Maleev, in 1954.

CLASSIFICATION: Saurischia, Theropoda, Therizinosauridae.

REMAINS: discovered in Asia.

DIMENSIONS: length: 7 metres
height: 3 metres
weight: 3 tonnes.

FOOD: herbivore?

CHARACTERISTICS: *Therizinosaurus* was a strange biped dinosaur. It had a small head, a long neck, a short tail and a large body. It had enormous front limbs and hands with three digits. The nails were incredibly long, shaped like claws and over 70 centimetres in length. But perhaps *Therizinosaurus* was an innocuous dinosaur; some scientists believe that it used its claws just to cut the grass and gather the leaves and shoots on which it fed, or perhaps to hold on to the branches of a tree to help it reach its favourite fruit and leaves.

Did you know that...

Therizinosaurus was an unusual theropod dinosaur which, unlike all the other dinosaurs in the group, probably ate both vegetation and meat. It is possible that its body may have been covered by feathers because fossil remains of Beipiaosaurus, a close relative of Therizinosaurus, show the impression of primitive feathers on its skin.

DINO QUIZ:

How long were the forelimbs of *Therizinosaurus*?

Its forelimbs were 2.5 metres long.

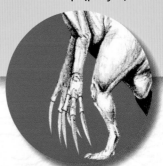

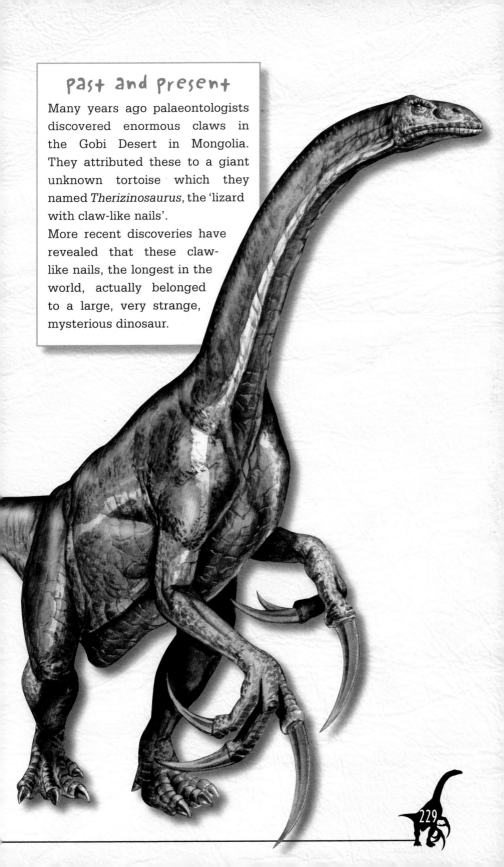

past and present

Many years ago palaeontologists discovered enormous claws in the Gobi Desert in Mongolia. They attributed these to a giant unknown tortoise which they named *Therizinosaurus*, the 'lizard with claw-like nails'.

More recent discoveries have revealed that these claw-like nails, the longest in the world, actually belonged to a large, very strange, mysterious dinosaur.

TRICERATOPS

NAME: *Triceratops* means 'three-horned face'.

DISCOVERED BY: Marsh, in 1889.

CLASSIFICATION: Ornithischia, Marginocephalia, Ceratopsidae.

REMAINS: discovered in North America.

DIMENSIONS: length: 9 metres
height: 3 metres
weight: 6 tonnes.

FOOD: herbivore.

CHARACTERISTICS: *Triceratops* was the largest ceratopsid. At the back of its head it had an enormous bony frill, 2 metres wide with a crested edge, while its skull had three horns: two at the top and one on the nose. It probably used its horns to defend itself against predators but also when fighting with other males. The bony frill not only protected its back and neck but also provided an excellent anchorage for powerful masticatory muscles; some scientists believe that this frill may have been brightly coloured to attract the females. Its snout ended in a beak like that of a parrot to enable it to cut tough vegetation; the jaws themselves were densely lined with teeth for chewing. It had a massive body and very powerful legs to support its weight while running but, based on its size, it is not thought that *Triceratops* could have been a fast runner.

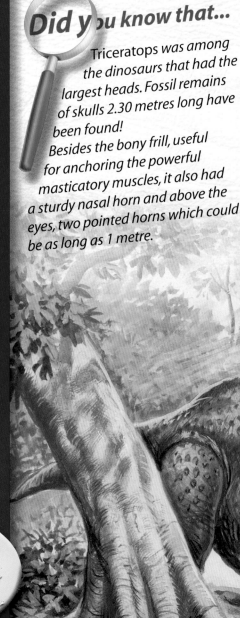

Did you know that...

*Triceratops was among the dinosaurs that had the largest heads. Fossil remains of skulls 2.30 metres long have been found!
Besides the bony frill, useful for anchoring the powerful masticatory muscles, it also had a sturdy nasal horn and above the eyes, two pointed horns which could be as long as 1 metre.*

NOW, AS THEN ...

Triceratops is reminiscent of today's rhinoceros. Even their way of life was probably very similar.

When threatened by a predator, *Triceratops* would defend itself by charging as a rhinoceros would do today. *Triceratops* lived in very large herds and, in case of danger, the adults would position themselves in a circle with their horns pointing outwards, thus protecting their young in the middle.

DINO QUIZ:

Why are so many *Triceratops* fossil skeletons found close to each other?

Triceratops lived in herds and migrated enormous distances. If they had to cross a river on their journey many animals could drown together. The muddy sediments of a large river are ideal for fossilisation which is why many fossilised *Triceratops* skeletons have been found close to each other.

TROODON

NAME: *Troodon* means 'tooth which hurts'.

DISCOVERED BY: Leidy, in 1856.

CLASSIFICATION: Saurischia, Theropoda, Troodontidae.

REMAINS: discovered in North America.

DIMENSIONS: length: 2 metres
height: 1 metre
weight: 60 kilograms.

FOOD: carnivore.

CHARACTERISTICS: *Troodon* was a small biped dinosaur, a lithe, fast predator which used its rigid tail to keep its balance. It had very long legs and claw-like nails. Its forelimbs were well developed and it had claws at the end of its fingers, the first finger being opposed to the other two. *Troodon* had a very large skull which indicates that it had a well-developed brain and was one of the most intelligent dinosaurs. Its teeth were sharp, curved, and serrated along the edges. It had large eyes which suggests it had sharp vision and was probably an excellent night hunter.

Did you know that...

In the 1980s the Canadian palaeontologist Dale Russel studied the fossils of Troodon, which at the time was classified as Stenonychosaurus and tried to imagine how this very intelligent dinosaur would have evolved if it had not become extinct. Russel conceived and produced a possible model of a 'dinosaurid', halfway between a reptile and a human, which is on display at the National Museum of Natural Sciences in Ottawa. The dinosaurid would have had a biped, erect posture, without a tail (this being no longer needed to maintain its balance). It would have had large eyes, hands with three opposable digits with claws, a large skull containing a highly developed brain and a skin covered with scales. The females would not have laid eggs but given birth to well-formed young which, since they were unable to breastfeed like mammals, they would have fed by regurgitating their food to them.

DINO QUIZ:

Is it possible that _Troodon_ would also have had feathers?

Troodon is part of a group called maniraptors, from which birds are descended; as a result many scientists believe they may have been feathered.

NOW, AS THEN ...

Troodon hunted at night and ate small animals such as primitive mammals, frogs, birds and small reptiles. The type of prey it favoured and its hunting technique remind us of the **fox** today.

233

TURIASAURUS

latest · discovery ·

NAME: The name *Turiasaurus* means 'Turia lizard'. Turia is the Latin name of the Spanish province of Teruel where it was first discovered.

DISCOVERED BY: Royo-Torres, in 2006.

CLASSIFICATION: Saurischia, Sauropoda, Diplodocidae.

REMAINS: discovered in Europe.

DIMENSIONS: length: 27 metres
height: 9 metres
weight: 48 tonnes.

FOOD: herbivore.

CHARACTERISTICS: *Turiasaurus* was an enormous quadruped dinosaur with columnar legs. It fed on vegetation, like all sauropods and had a very small head but a very long neck and tail.

Did you know that...

Turiasaurus *was only discovered very recently and is the largest dinosaur so far found in Europe. It was discovered in Spain, near the town of Riodeva, through the work of the palaeontologist Rafael Royo-Torres of the Joint Paleontology Foundation of Teruel-Dinopolis.*

DINO QUIZ:

How long was the humerus of *Turiasaurus*?

The humerus, the longest bone in the front limb, was 1.79 metres long: as long as an adult human is tall!

Past and Present

The well-preserved, almost complete skeleton of the *Turiasaurus* was used to create a bio-mechanical model to try and help scientists understand how large animals with a spinal column tens of metres long would have moved.

235

TYRANNOSAURUS

NAME: *Tyrannosaurus* means 'tyrant lizard'.

DISCOVERED BY: Osborn, in 1905.

CLASSIFICATION: Saurischia, Theropoda, Tyrannosauridae.

REMAINS: discovered in North America.

DIMENSIONS: length: 14 metres
height: 6 metres
weight: 7 tonnes.

FOOD: carnivore.

CHARACTERISTICS: *Tyrannosaurus* was a gigantic carnivorous dinosaur. It had a massive, elongated skull over 1.50 metres long; the muscles of its jaws were extremely strong and its neck so powerful that it could drag heavy prey and tear off large chunks of flesh from it. *Tyrannosaurus* moved only on its hind legs which were very muscular, strong and long enough to enable it to run quite fast. In contrast its forelimbs were very small with only two digits. This was probably so as not to weigh down the front part of the body further, which was already supporting its massive skull. Possibly it used these short forelimbs, which were too short even to carry food to its mouth, to help it get off the ground when lying down. *Tyrannosaurus* had over 50 teeth which were enormous, some as much as 20 centimetres long, and had serrated edges. They were very sharp, curved inwards and could tear a prey to pieces and rip kilograms of flesh off the carcass in a single bite. But palaeontologists disagree about the hunting technique of *Tyrannosaurus*. Some believe it hunted by chasing its prey while others think that it laid ambushes and traps. Others again hold that it fed only on carrion or that it snatched the prey caught by other animals. Given its enormous size, it may not have been able to pursue a prey for a long time. It is more likely that it just attacked and snatched its prey and then waited for it to die.

Did you know that...

Tyrannosaurus *was one of the most fearsome, terrifying predators that ever lived on Earth. Its prey included ceratopsids (on some bones of which traces of* Tyrannosaurus *teeth have been observed) as well as hadrosaurs: fragments of* Edmontosaurus *bones have been discovered in some* Tyrannosaurus *coprolite (fossilised excrement).*

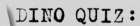

DINO QUIZ:

What recent discoveries have been made about the young of *Tyrannosaurus*?

According to the most recent discoveries, *Tyrannosaurus* young were born with a thick layer of feathers to keep them warm. The feathers gradually disappeared as they grew up.

236

past and present

For almost a century *Tyrannosaurus* has been recognised as the largest carnivorous dinosaur that ever existed but other specimens of dinosaur recently discovered in Africa and South America are even larger! *Carcharodontosaurus*, found in North Africa, weighed eight tons. Its skull was even bigger than that of *Tyrannosaurus* and its teeth are reminiscent of those of a shark. *Gigantosaurus* which lived in South America was bigger than both of them.

Carcharodontosaurus could weigh a tonne more than *Tyrannosaurus*.

ULTRASAUROS

NAME: *Ultrasauros* means 'ultra lizard'.

DISCOVERED BY: Jensen and Olshevsky, in 1991.

CLASSIFICATION: Saurischia, Sauropoda, Brachiosauridae.

REMAINS: discovered in North America.

DIMENSIONS: length: 30 metres
height: 15 metres
weight: 80 tonnes.

FOOD: herbivore.

CHARACTERISTICS: *Ultrasauros* was a gigantic sauropod. It had four enormous columnar legs which supported all its weight and it moved as a quadruped. The hind legs were shorter than the front ones. Its extremely long neck enabled it to reach the most tender young leaves on the top of the tallest trees which it tore off with its razor-sharp teeth. *Ultrasauros* was obliged to eat continuously because it needed enormous quantities of vegetation in order to survive. It also ate small stones, called gastroliths which were moved by the muscles of the digestive system, helping to grind the food, thus facilitating digestion. *Ultrasauros* lived in herds which roamed in search of pastures. It defended itself against predators by discouraging them with its size and threatening them with the sharp claws on its feet and its long tail which it used as a whip.

Did you know that...

Ultrasauros, *together with* Supersaurus *and* Brachiosaurus, *was one of the tallest, fattest, heaviest dinosaurs that ever lived on our planet. Some scientists believe that* Ultrasauros *actually belongs to the* Brachiosaurus *genus of which it would be a new, larger species.*

DINO QUIZ:

Are _Ultrasauros_ and _Ultrasaurus_ two slightly different names for the same dinosaur?

No, _Ultrasauros_ is an American sauropod and should not be confused with _Ultrasaurus_, that ends in '-us' instead of '-os', and is another large sauropod, discovered in South Korea.

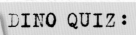

NOW, AS THEN ...

Ultrasauros was as large as a group of 25 **giraffes**.

239

UTAHRAPTOR

NAME: *Utahraptor* means 'Utah's predator', and is named after the American State in which it was discovered.

DISCOVERED BY: Kirkland, Burge and Gaston, in 1993.

CLASSIFICATION: Saurischia, Theropoda, Dromaeosauridae.

REMAINS: discovered in North America.

DIMENSIONS: length: 7 metres
height: 2 metres
weight: 700 kilograms.

FOOD: carnivore.

CHARACTERISTICS: *Utahraptor* had large eyes, long forelimbs and strong hands with claws and wrists which it could bend to grab or hold onto larger prey. Its hind legs were long and powerful which enabled it to jump and leap; its feet also had claws. *Utahraptor* is known for killing its prey not with its teeth but with the curved, retractable claw on its second toe. To keep its balance when standing on one leg and kicking with the other, it used its tail which was structured to work as a counterweight and stiffened by long tendons.

Did you know that...

Utahraptor is the largest representative of the family of dromeosaurs which includes the famous Velociraptor and Deynonychus; it was an agile, fast, astute dinosaur which hunted even large prey in herds.

past and present

In his film **Jurassic Park**, Steven Spielberg included among the dinosaur participants a dromeosaur which was called *Velociraptor* in the story.

Its large size makes the dromeosaur very similar to *Utahraptor* which had not yet been found when the film was made but which would shortly be discovered.

DINO QUIZ:

How long were the two long, curved claws of *Utahraptor*?

These long, curved claws were almost 30 centimetres long.

VELOCIRAPTOR

NAME: The name *Velociraptor* means 'swift thief'.

DISCOVERED BY: Osborn, in 1924.

CLASSIFICATION: Saurischia, Theropoda, Dromaeosauridae.

REMAINS: discovered in Asia.

DIMENSIONS: length: 1.80 metres
height: 1 metre
weight: 15 kilograms.

FOOD: carnivore.

CHARACTERISTICS: *Velociraptor* was a small dromeosaur and was a very agile biped. It had long limbs, an S-shaped neck, an elongated head, a flattened muzzle and sharp teeth curved inwards. It did not kill its prey with its teeth but with the lethal claw-shaped nail on its second toe. *Velociraptor* kept this sharp, curved nail raised when walking and running but when the animal attacked and kicked, extending its leg, the nail automatically opened out like a pocket knife. Meanwhile, its hind legs could deliver powerful kicks so that its claws ripped open its prey.
Velociraptor could also jump very well because its long, rigid tail helped it keep its balance. It had long forelimbs and hands whose digits had claws; it could rotate its wrists laterally to hold its prey more easily.

Did you know that...

Velociraptor is a well known dinosaur and the structure of its skeleton suggests that it was agile and fast. High-energy motor performances such as jumping, running, kicking and really dast sprinting require a lot of energy which only a warm-blooded animal could have.

Many palaeontologists are now convinced that small and energetic dinosaurs such as Velociraptor, *must have had warm blood. In this case* Velociraptor *must have been able to insulate its body from changes in temperature; it is therefore probable that it was covered with feathers.*

Detail of the hind leg of *Velociraptor*.

DINO QUIZ:

Did *Velociraptor* hunt alone or in groups?

It is thought that *Velociraptor* could hunt small prey on its own but it would hunt in a group if the prey was much larger than itself.

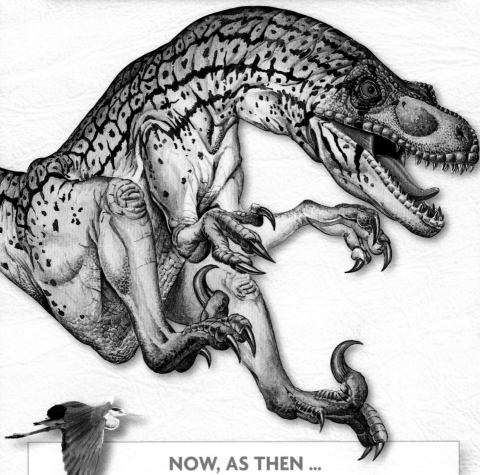

NOW, AS THEN ...

The wrists of *Velociraptor* could make a lateral rotating movement to help it hold its prey. **Birds** are able to make a similar movement which is essential for manoeuvring the wings while flying. This similarity is not surprising since *Velociraptors* are among the closest relatives of the birds.

243

WUERHOSAURUS

NAME: *Wuerhosaurus* means 'Wuerho lizard', after the Chinese locality where it was discovered.

DISCOVERED BY: Dong Zhiming, in 1973.

CLASSIFICATION: Ornithischia, Tyreophora, Stegosauridae.

REMAINS: discovered in Asia.

DIMENSIONS: length: 8 metres
height: 1.80 metres
weight: 4 tonnes.

FOOD: herbivore.

CHARACTERISTICS: *Wuerhosaurus* was a massive quadruped dinosaur. It had a shorter body and wider sides than the other stegosaurs. The head was small and elongated; it walked with its head very close to the soil so as to feed more easily on low-growing vegetation. It had osseous rounded plates on its back and four spikes on the end of its tail which it used as a defensive weapon.

Did you know that...

Wuerhosaurus is one of the rare stegosaurs which survived until the beginning of the Cretaceous period. It had strange bony plates on its back which were rather short and rounded, different from those of the other stegosaurs

The tail of *Wuerhosaurus* was a lethal weapon thanks to its four sharply pointed spikes.

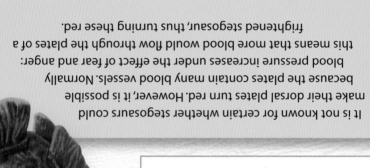

DINO QUIZ:

Is it true that the plates on the back of stegosaurs could turn red to frighten predators?

It is not known for certain whether stegosaurs could make their dorsal plates turn red. However, it is possible because the plates contain many blood vessels. Normally blood pressure increases under the effect of fear and anger: this means that more blood would flow through the plates of a frightened stegosaur, thus turning these red.

past and present

The very few fossil remains which have been discovered have been attributed to two different species: *Wuerhosaurus homheni* – about 8 metres long and found in China in the province of Xinjiang – and the slightly smaller *Wuerhosaurus ordosensis*, found in Mongolia.

245

XIAOSAURUS

NAME: *Xiaosaurus* means 'small lizard'.

DISCOVERED BY: Dong Zhiming and Tang Zilu, in 1983.

CLASSIFICATION: Ornithischia, Ornithopoda, Fabrosauridae.

REMAINS: discovered in China.

DIMENSIONS: length: 1.50 metres
height: 50 centimetres.

FOOD: herbivore.

CHARACTERISTICS: *Xiaosaurus* was a small, fast-running, agile dinosaur. It walked on its two long hind legs; its feet had four digits while the hands on its short arms had five digits. It had a long, rigid tail, a flexible neck and a small head with large eyes and serrated, leaf-shaped teeth.

Did you know that...

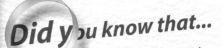

Xiaosaurus is probably a member of the fabrosaur family, primitive ornithopods which could be the ancestors of all subsequent ornithischian dinosaurs.

Xiaosaurus was a herbivorous biped dinosaur.

Past and Present

Xiaosaurus is known only through the discovery of a few teeth and some isolated bones. Its remains are too few and fragmentary to enable palaeontologists to classify it accurately.

DINO QUIZ:

How many million years ago did *Xiaosaurus* live?

Xiaosaurus lived about 165 million years ago in the Middle Jurassic period.

YANGCHUANOSAURUS

NAME: *Yangchuanosaurus* means 'Lizard of Yang-ch'uan', a locality in north-eastern China.

DISCOVERED BY: Dong Zhiming, in 1978.

CLASSIFICATION: Saurischia, Theropoda, Sinraptoridae.

REMAINS: discovered in Asia.

DIMENSIONS: length: 10 metres
height: 4 metres
weight: 3 tonnes.

FOOD: carnivore.

CHARACTERISTICS: *Yangchuanosaurus* was a large biped carnosaur. It had a large head over 1.10 metres long and powerful jaws with serrated teeth. It had two low crests which were possibly brightly coloured. It had a massive neck, short forelimbs and a kind of low sail on its back which ran from the neck to the tail.
Its hind legs were muscular and its feet had sharp claws.

Did you know that...

Yangchuanosaurus is described as the Asian allosaur because it was the largest predator of its time in the region which today lies in north-eastern China.

DINO QUIZ:

What was special about the tail of *Yangchuanosaurus*?

The tail of *Yangchuanosaurus* was about half the length of its whole body.

past and present

Yangchuanosaurus was discovered in 1978 but it was only in 1993, after the discovery of a specimen of *Sinraptor* related to it, that it became possible to classify it accurately in the new family of Sinraptoridae.

ZEPHYROSAURUS

NAME: *Zephyrosaurus* means 'Zephyr's lizard', after the god of the west wind in Greek mythology.

DISCOVERED BY: H. D. Sues, in 1980.

CLASSIFICATION: Ornithischia, Ornithopoda, Hypsilophodontidae.

REMAINS: discovered in North America.

DIMENSIONS: length: 1.8 metres
height: 90 centimetres.

FOOD: herbivore.

CHARACTERISTICS: *Zephyrosaurus* was a small biped dinosaur. It had an unusually shaped skull and teeth in the front part of its mouth. Its hind legs were long and slender, while its forelimbs were short.

Did you know that...

Today it is known as Zephyrosaurus after the discovery of a part of a fossilised skull and a few bones in Montana in the 1980s.

New remains have recently been found which come from at least seven animals and include bones from more or less all parts of the body. These new Zephyrosaurus fossilised remains have been studied since 2003 at the Sam Noble Oklahoma Museum of Natural History. In 2004 fossilised footprints were discovered in Maryland and Virginia which, based on the proportions of the hands and feet, would also seem to belong to Zephyrosaurus.

NOW, AS THEN:

It is the condition of their teeth which has suggested to scientists that *Zephyrosaurus* had the capability of moving its jaws sideways to the right and left as well as up and down. This will have enabled it to 'chew' its food, although not with the complex movements and efficiency of today's **ruminants**.

DINO QUIZ:

In which phase of the Cretaceous period did *Zephyrosaurus* live?

In the Lower Cretaceous period between 119 and 113 million years ago.

Index of

MANIRAPTORS

PRIMITIVE
THERAPODS

CARNOSAURS

ORNITHOMIMIDS

CERATOSAURIDS

SAUROPODS

ORNITHOPODS

inosaurs

PACHICEPHALOSAURIDS

CERATOPSIDS

STEGOSAURIDS

ANCHYLOSAURIDS

FEATHERED
DINOSAURS

THERIZINOSAURIDS